Logic

The Truth About Blacks
And The Republican Party

And Why They Need To Work Together
To Improve The Party,
The Black Community,
And The Country

C. Douglas Love

For more information visit:
www.thinkordie.org

This book is dedicated to my beloved wife, Sophia
Everything I am, everything I do, and everything
I'll ever become is better because of you

Contents

"Any refusal to recognize reality, for any reason whatever, has disastrous consequences. There are no evil thoughts except one: the refusal to think."

Ayn Rand – *Atlas Shrugged*

Preface

" **I**'m a Democrat." I have never *really* uttered those words, but then, I've never had to. We can all assume that it's a given, right? I'm Black and I grew up in a working-class household in one of the poorest cities in America. As a child, most of the families I knew were either of the working class or on welfare. So, of course — I'm a Democrat. I have always been told that they were the party who had my best interests at heart, and I had no reason to doubt it.

I grew up in Gary, Indiana, a city that at the time had a minority population of 89% and a political machine rivaling that of Chicago. Every politician in the city and county was a Democrat. Even the governorship, controlled by Republicans since 1969, had been taken over by the Democrats from the time I became eligible to vote in 1989 until 2005. This is important to note, as it left me nothing with which to compare the Democrats and no way to challenge the things I had always been told about the Republicans. I didn't have a chance. I compare it to a White child growing up being told only negative things about Blacks but not having any Blacks in his life to combat those views. It would be nearly impossible for that child not to grow up believing stereotypes about Blacks. This was the case with my views on Republicans.

When I was in my mid-twenties and starting to pay attention to politics, I realized that I never really had been a Democrat. At the very least I was an Independent, and I believe that this is the case for about a third of the country's voting population. There are those voters who agree completely and wholeheartedly on every issue with the Democrats or Republicans, but this is rare. Most people have some Liberal and Conservative views, and those views will vary based on the issues. In spite of this, there are some groups whose choice of party supersedes their beliefs and stance on the issues. Hispanics, Jews, women, and White males all vote in greater numbers for one party over the other, often in direct contrast to their beliefs. However, there is only one group that votes almost entirely for one party: the Black community.

Much of this has to do with the tendency of Blacks to base their views on emotion. Because of their reliance on emotion, they allow their perceptions to cloud reality, and for Blacks, these perceptions usually have to do with race. We perceive one party to be working to help our race and the other working to destroy it. The reality is far more gray than black and white (pun intended) and far less sinister. The stereotypes Blacks believe about Republicans cannot be logically applied to the majority of the party; however, these stereotypes are powerful and lead many to vote for Democrats regardless of their stance on any issue.

It is clear that the country is divided on the issues, and the Black community is no exception. Based on issues alone, there is at least 35% of the population on either side of every issue. Gun control, gay marriage, the economy — you name it, if you poll the entire country, no less than 35% would oppose or support almost any issue. The poll would have very similar results if done solely in the Black community. For example, if the issue in the poll was gun control, the results would be about 65/35 with 35% being against stricter gun control. You could go on, issue by issue, and never get less than 25% of the Black population to agree with either side of the position. However, the Republicans will never get anywhere near 25% of the Black vote. Why is that? This is proof that, for many, party affiliation is not driven by the issues. Most of it has to do with perception.

If you ask Black people their perception of Republicans or the Republican Party, most will say that the Republicans protect big business and put capitalism ahead of what's best for the citizens, that they are religious zealots trying to control social issues, or that they are racists. Once these ideas about Republicans were put into their minds, no one had a reason to challenge them. These ideas became facts and not just opinions. This leads to one simple question, "What if they are wrong?" For years, Blacks have assumed that the Democrats were working in their best interest. They had so much faith in the Democrats that they doubled down on them by buying into the rhetoric of the racist Republican. What if Blacks are wrong about Republicans being racists or wrong about the Democrats' plans being best for them? Either way, this would be bad, since the Black community has already conceded their power by casting a monolithic vote for Democrats.

I have never written a book before, but I was compelled to write this book after the 2012 presidential campaign began. For as far back as I can remember, the Republicans have been perceived within the Black community as being unhelpful with regards to their specific problems. Since the election of the country's first non-White president, Republicans have basically been equated to the Klan. Every disagreement they voice against the president has been deemed racially motivated. This has caused Blacks to wrongfully assume the worst of every Republican and has left the Republicans at a loss on how to address legitimate concerns and how to communicate their views in an inclusive manner. This book will serve as a direct plea to both groups.

First, I'd like to address the Black community. I understand that most Blacks are self-described Democrats and that many honestly believe in the Democratic platform; however, there are many Blacks whose beliefs are aligned with the Republican ideals but won't listen to the Republicans' arguments due to perceptions they've learned over the years. I am hopeful that reading the logical analysis here will lead them to read, listen, observe, and finally seek out their own individual political alliance. The goal isn't to make them Republicans; it's only to stop them from blindly following others and to help them understand that the "Democrats are good and Republicans are bad" approach to political issues is a gross oversimplification that has been detrimental to the Black community. I also hope that those in the Black community who don't change their views will allow other Blacks to embrace their Conservatism and openly join the Republican Party without succumbing to the character assassinations that are currently assigned to Black Republicans.

Next, I will address the Republican Party, particularly White Republicans. Let's face it; the majority of Republicans, at least the people who admit it, are White and are completely at a loss when it comes to how to get their message across to minorities. Though they share core beliefs with many of them, they continue to alienate them. I can only assume that they would want to attract as many votes as possible. Even those Republicans who are racists have to see the advantage in gaining additional votes, as the Democrats have for years. I hope that by reading this book, Republicans will learn how they are perceived and realize that until they overcome these negative views and dispel them, where they stand on the issues won't matter because many will not consider their ideas. I will also give specific directions on how they should adjust their message and where they need to go to get it out there.

This is not the first book written about the relationship between the Black community and the Republican Party, but there are two significant differences that make this book unique. The first is that the other books are written about specific issues and attempt to point out flaws in the other party while making the writer's party seem innocent if not angelic in its goal to help the country. The authors tend to come off as mean and often use words such as "stupid" or "liar" in their titles. This delivery method turns people off.

The approach here is to look at it from an Independent point of view, and while some might say I'm advocating for the Republican Party, that is only because in explaining why a misconception is wrong I have to state an alternative view and point out why that argument is illogical. However, I do not resort to the 'We're good and they're bad' argument that other books use. I assume positive intent. I believe that the majority of politicians in both parties want to improve things and simply differ in their approach. This book will not be an all-out indictment of the Democrats or a full embrace of the Republicans. The topic should be observed from a broader view, focusing on the beliefs, behaviors, lies, stereotypes, and misconceptions that make it difficult for the two groups to work together.

The other difference, possibly the most intriguing, is how I differ from other Black Conservative authors. Many of the Black Conservatives who have penned books or who serve as political pundits on TV are viewed as rich. Most are Ivy League college graduates, are tenured professors, or are entrepreneurs with successful businesses. They are not viewed as 'average Blacks', so many in the Black community feel they cannot relate to them. This plays into the stereotypes that all Black Republicans are elitists who have achieved a certain level of status and therefore don't care about those who are struggling. While this is unfair, I don't fall into any of the above categories and am, by all measurements, an ordinary guy. I simply don't believe that being a non-rich Black man should automatically decide my political affiliation or that a Black person identifying as a Republican or a Conservative should have his or her Blackness questioned.

I hope that people will begin to use logic over emotion when evaluating issues. It is also important to note that there won't be a point-by-point synopsis of the major issues and how each party believes they should be addressed. While there may be some topics used as examples, I want the focus to be on dispelling mistruths and on improving communications between the two groups, not on specific issues or who is right or wrong on a particular issue. The conversations brought forth by this book should be about how people choose sides and not which side they choose.

The goal is to invoke an open and honest discussion about race and politics. While most of the focus will be on Blacks and the Republican Party, these issues and the suggested solutions apply to other groups as well. The Black community serves as the test group because they vote against Republicans in the greatest numbers. If Blacks can overcome their perception of Republicans, and if Republicans can find a way to make inroads with them, then that success could easily be duplicated with other groups. If I can get the Republicans to actively defend themselves against these misconceptions while simultaneously convincing Blacks that remaining open to ideas from Republicans will be beneficial for their community, then my work will be done.

Part I

FOUNDATION

Childhood

As did many poor Blacks, my mom grew up in a segregated neighborhood and lived her entire life in the same town. She was born and raised in Gary, Indiana. Her parents split early in her childhood, and though she kept a good relationship with her father, she was raised by her mother. Most of the places they called home were more like slums. Though she recalled a time when the city's downtown was bustling and the economy was robust, she noted that it was segregated and the predominately Black area was a 180-degree experience from the rest of the city. She remembers having no utilities at times and living in filthy conditions. She told me that Blacks were threatened or attacked for being in certain areas or out too late. She described what it felt like to not be allowed to shop in some stores or try on clothes in others. Basically, 1950s Gary, Indiana was just like Alabama or Mississippi but with a different climate. This definitely molded her views of Whites. Even when she spoke of Whites who were nice to her, she made it clear that they were exceptions to the rule.

I know very little about my father's early childhood. He was born in Oklahoma in 1920 but that is all I know about his life prior to his high school days in East Chicago, Indiana. My father was a good student, but just before graduating high school, he found out that he was going to be a father. He married his high school sweetheart, and in 1939 my half-sister Frances was born. After graduating high school, he enlisted in the Army where he served admirably during WW II. Shortly after returning home, he and his wife divorced. After completing his service, he worked with his friend doing odd jobs such as home and auto repair. They had a little makeshift shop in Gary, and it was there that he met my mother. She was working as a caregiver at the time. They dated for a few years and married in 1963. On January 13, 1964, my brother Ronald was born. By this time my father had secured a job in the steel mill. When my mother became pregnant with their second child, my parents decided that she would stay home to take care of the children. My mother would not return to work and went on to have two more children; Leroy, the middle child, and myself, the youngest. My parents were together for 37 years until my father's death in July of 2000.

Throughout my childhood, my parents guided me and taught me fundamental lessons that remain with me to this day. I am thankful for that foundation, because by the time I became a teenager, I began to notice that my mother's views didn't exactly match up to what she had taught me. Over time, it became clear that my parents both had different experiences growing up which had led to vastly different views on race. Given the most basic information about them, one would think that my mom would have had more open views than my dad. After all, his father had been the president of the local chapter of the NAACP, and while my father was 16 years my mother's senior and from Oklahoma, she was from a large northern city and her father was of mixed race. However, things started to come into focus as I matured and started to ask questions.

I have to give my mom a huge amount of credit for putting parenting above her own views. Despite how she felt, she made it a point to allow me to form my own opinions. I remember her telling me to listen, think, and question everything and everybody, even her. She said, "Even I can be wrong about some things." Occasionally, she would make comments when she got upset about something, but for the most part she tried to keep her views to herself. If it had not been for her restraint, who knows what my views on race would be?

When I was about eight years old, our family took a trip to Rochester, Minnesota to the Mayo Clinic. My brother was suffering from severe asthma and eczema, so my parents took him to the clinic to see a specialist. Though this was a very serious time and my parents were worried, they did a great job of making this more of a vacation than a medical trip. We got to stay in a hotel and do some sightseeing. The visits to the clinic felt more like breaks in our vacation than a somber occasion. Soon, the visits also became part of our vacation. My brother met a boy who was there being treated for similar ailments as he was. They spent their time between doctor visits playing together. Then they were given an unbelievable opportunity. Chicago Bears' quarterback Vince Evans was there visiting children at the hospital. My brother and his new friend got to interview him, and it was broadcast throughout the hospital, making them stars to everyone there. After they were released from the hospital, our family went to stay with the boy's family for a couple of days. We had a great time. Later, I found out that when the family extended the offer for us to visit, my father thought it would be a positive end to our trip, but my mother didn't want to because she didn't want to stay at the home of these, "Strange White people." This would not be the last time she suppressed her feelings on race for the sake of her children.

During summer breaks, we would take road trips to visit my paternal grandmother and her second husband. For most of my childhood, they lived in Dalhart, TX. Dalhart was the antithesis of Gary, which was a populous, urban city with approximately 150,000 people, 84% of whom were Black. Dalhart was an arid and desolate rural town with less than 10,000 residents, and 85% of its population was White. I remember things being slower and looking very different from what they were like back in Gary. However, once we met the other children and started to play, all of the differences seemed to disappear. We played the same games, pretended to be the same superheroes, and got into the same silly fights.

Because we visited on a regular basis, we got to know many of the neighboring families. Our annual visits gave us another set of friends. Almost all of the kids we played with were White, and we didn't have any problems for years. One of the last summers we visited, we reconnected with some of the kids we knew in the neighborhood. One of them introduced us to a new kid. We hung out most of that day, but the next day, when we got together, the new kid wasn't there. I asked if he was coming and my friend told me the kid's parents told him they couldn't play together as long as I was there. When I got home, I told my dad and said I didn't understand. He told me, "There are just some people who will dislike you without knowing you." He said, "They are wrong, and their attitude only represents a

6

small number of people. Most people are good, but you have to be mindful of those who are not, without being prejudice against an entire group of people." He asked, "If a Black person stole from you, would you think all Black people were thieves?" I said, "No." He said, "The same goes for Whites. Someone may be racist against you, but you know that is not how all White people are. Try to judge people individually." This is something I continue to live by today.

My father was not a vocal person. He had very few 'heart-to-hearts' like this with us. When a situation arose, he dealt with it head on. Other than that, there were very few discussions. Most of what my brothers and I learned from him came through his actions and the examples he set. Neither of my parents were strict disciplinarians, nor did they try to become our friends. My dad, however, was more set in his ways than my mom. He was older than most parents who had children my age, having married my mother later in life. When I was born, my father was 51. By the time I started to develop friendships, I noticed that he was the same age as many of my friends' grandparents. This explains some of the more traditional views he tried to instill in me when I was growing up.

He would wake me early in the morning on Saturdays to assist him with his weekly odd jobs. He was very handy and believed it was necessary for a man to be able to fix things. He made me help him with a variety of tasks, such as fixing a leak, patching drywall, or working on the car. I hated it! It felt like punishment!

I understand now that he was trying to teach me, but, at the time, all I wanted to do was sleep late on Saturdays. He asked me when I was about twelve years old, "What are you going to do if your car breaks down?" I laughed, internally of course, and said, "I'm going to hire someone to fix it."

Later, when I went away to school, my father gave me $100 and told me I was now a man and therefore on my own. We were definitely not rich, but I'm not sure how much financial assistance he would have given me if we were. He felt that he had made it through life on his own and that for me to appreciate my success, I'd have to do the same.

There came a time when I needed to borrow some money from him. He gave it to me and said, "I only borrowed money from an individual once, my dad, and I paid him back immediately. You never want to owe anyone." In addition to the things he told me, I learned a lot by watching him. I learned the importance of hard work, not to blame others for your shortcomings, and the importance of responsibility. I also got a lesson on race I didn't realize I was getting at the time. Though we never spoke about race, it became obvious that he didn't have the same apprehensions that my mother had about Whites. The first glaring difference was that my father had White friends.

Of all the things that could have been said about my hometown, the most obvious couldn't be seen until you looked from the outside. I didn't notice how 'Black' Gary was until I went away to school. When I was a child, with the exception of a few teachers, I could go the entire day and never see a White person. The mayor, the councilmen, the police chief, store clerks, etc. were all Black. Since my summers in Dalhart had been when I was so much younger, I didn't notice the difference. Therefore, when my father introduced me to his White friends, often in an avuncular manner, it stood out. This was primarily because I'd never met White people any other way.

When my mom would make comments about White people, my dad would tell me, "You can't use that as a basis to judge people." When my father died in 2000, we were going through his things and found his high school yearbook. Though dated, it was similar to high school yearbooks you see today — most likely to succeed, most popular, class clown, etc. In addition, there were many notes and well wishes from classmates. My father seemed to be popular, as there were kind words from many of his classmates, but this was no surprise. What surprised me was the fact that over half of his classmates were White. This was from a graduating class in 1939.

In spite of my parents' differences, our household was relatively peaceful. I am sure my parents fought sometimes. I would learn later from my mom that it was more often than I would have imagined, but they never let us see it. They were principled but not in an overt way, loving but not overly affectionate, and strict but not enough to promote rebellion. They were driven to help us succeed and become well-rounded but didn't make us feel pressured.

For my entire childhood, maintaining the home and the development of the children was my mother's job. She made sure she kept our time occupied. She was a lover of music and wanted us to be exposed to many different things. We all had to take piano lessons. We enjoyed sports, so we were encouraged to play. In addition to my father making me help with household work on the weekends, my mother enrolled me in a Saturday school program that I stayed in from second grade until I started junior high. She would always say that she wasn't smart but wouldn't allow that to limit our growth. When we mentioned what we were interested in, my parents tried to foster it. When I was in sixth grade, my father retired from the mill. This gave us an unusual dynamic at home.

When my brothers and I were very young, most of our friends lived with both parents. It was still relatively rare to see single parents, and when it did happen, it was considered an unfortunate situation. By the time I started high school, I had both parents at home all the time, while most of my friends were now being raised by one parent, in most cases their working mothers, leaving no adult at home for most of the day.

Education was important, but I don't believe my parents knew how to create a focus and set goals for us. As with many Black families in the '70s and '80s, we didn't have anyone in the family who had been to college. Because of this, my parents had no idea what they should do to get us into college, nor could they offer advice on what the experience would be like or how to succeed. This is a vital point that is sometimes overlooked and a major reason why children of college graduates are far more likely to go to college and graduate than children of non-college graduates. That being said, all three of us attended college immediately after graduating high school; however, none of us graduated (at least not immediately). Although the emphasis on college was not impressed specifically, my parents had a strong focus on us getting a good education.

My parents were not overtly religious. I knew they believed in God, but I never felt that they pushed us in any direction. My father would have Bible study with a traveling minister on weekends, but we weren't forced to attend. My mother didn't attend church very often. She would listen to Gospel music on Sundays and read the

Bible, but she never mentioned why she didn't go to church. None of this stopped us from having a religious foundation.

Helen Smith was our godmother, and we spent a considerable amount of time with her. She was a devout Christian, and at a young age, we started going to church every Sunday with her. We would participate in several church activities, and we began developing friendships with the other children. This is where my love of God and faith was developed; however, at home there was no shortage of life lessons and principles.

My godmother was also a caterer, and she allowed me to help her with some catering jobs, and her daughter, who was fourteen years my senior, helped expose me to new things. I started trying recipes, and, as in everything else, my mother encouraged me. At the time, I saw this simply as learning to cook, but it actually set the stage for me to accept new experiences without judging them first.

Then came the moment that had the biggest impact on me and changed the way I looked at everything. When I was little I loved music. It came from my mom. She always had music playing, and she would reminisce about how she went dancing all the time when she was younger. Like most Blacks in the 1970s, we listened to lots of Motown. My parents were older, so I was exposed to lots of Classic Jazz and Blues as well. In the early 1980s, around the time Disco was ending and Rap music was becoming popular, my musical tastes started to diversify. When MTV and *Friday Night Videos* started showing videos, the culture started to shift. The Pop music of the day was piped into homes across America, and there was no way to escape it. I thought I was being exposed to something new, but I had no idea how much I had been limited.

While growing up, one of my closest friends was Levi Mitchell. We had been friends since kindergarten and had started to develop a fondness for music together. He had an uncle who was a DJ, and we went to visit him. He had more records than I had ever seen, and he told us about the different types of events he did and that to be good he had to be diverse. He gave us some records to listen to and we left there wanting to be DJs. We went back to Levi's house and started to listen to the records. I had never heard anything like that before. Looking back, it's kind of funny; it was 1983 and I was experiencing some of the greatest bands ever for the first time, many of whom weren't even together anymore.

There were The Beatles, The Rolling Stones, Styx, and The Who, to name a few. We listened for hours. Finally, we got to the three artists that, for that moment, flicked a switch and changed how I processed everything around me. Jimi Hendrix, Led Zeppelin, and Kiss. Hendrix and Zeppelin made sense. After years of R&B, they were different but soulful enough to be a natural bridge into Rock. Kiss was different. Kiss was the group that stood out as straight Rock 'n' Roll with no clear lines to R&B, and all three groups did things musically that were new to me, so I wanted to hear more.

We continued to get music from Levi's uncle, but we also started to gather music on our own. The following summer, we got *Ride the Lighting*, a new album by a group called Metallica. I remember the first time we heard their music. They took Rock to a whole new level. We listened to the entire album with our mouths hanging open. We'd never heard a guitar played that way before and listened to "Fade to Black" over and over again. After this we wanted to be guitarists.

Observing, Listening, And Questioning

U p to this point, I had taken in a lot from my experiences. I realize that we are all products of our environment and that most Blacks are not brought up with an open mind to the world and the same experiences as I am. As these experiences were happening, I didn't see these things as different. When visiting Dalhart, trying new foods, or listening to Rock music, I was just having new experiences and enjoying them. At the same time that I was experiencing this growth, I was also hanging out with my friends and doing the things we had always done. Now that I was getting older, I started to see and hear how others thought, and I realized my views were different. Once I noticed this, I found myself observing everything and everyone around me. We all base our opinions on experiences, but when we are young and haven't had many experiences to rely on, our opinions are largely based on what we've been told and to what we've been exposed. As I was about to find out, my experiences were very different from most Black children my age, and it would bring about glaring differences in how we viewed the world.

The following year, I started high school, and you would think that I could not wait to share my newfound musical treasures. This is not exactly how things progressed. However, we did achieve one of our goals; we both started to DJ. Levi would go on to achieve both goals as he is currently the guitarist and lead singer of an L.A. based Rock band.[1] Oddly enough, we never mentioned our previous summers listening to Rock music. Since we were DJs now, we would mix in some of the more soulful songs by Rock artists with the House music and Rap that were becoming popular. Most went over okay with only an occasional leering eye. Still, most of my friends had no interest in hearing anything other than R&B, House music, and Rap. I distinctly remember a debate I had with a friend in high school. We were watching TV and some Pop and Rock videos came on. This is how our conversation went:

My friend: I don't like White music.

Me: What is White music?

My friend: Just that, music made by White people.

Me: Do you know that the Isley Brothers, Aretha Franklin, Marvin Gaye, and many others have all remade music originally performed by White artists?

My friend: It's not White music when *they* sing it.

She was convinced that Whites couldn't make good music, and nothing was going to change her mind. It's like the stereotype that Whites can't dance. If someone hasn't seen anything to prove the contrary, then he or she believes it as fact. Once this takes hold, giving them the stats of the large number of professional dancers who are White will have little effect in changing the views of those who have been convinced. I was starting to notice that close-minded views were very common and not limited to music or to school.

As we got older, we started to test the boundaries that our parents set for us, as many teens do. It was obvious that many of my friends had more freedom than I did. Fortunately, I had a brother two years my senior, and that enabled me to extend my curfew. By the time my brother graduated from high school, my friends had grown comfortable with doing what they wanted with limited supervision. Some of them would skip school without their parents' knowledge. To be honest, I probably would have also if I had thought I could get away with it. As we got busier working as DJs, I wanted to extend my curfew. My parents were split on what to do but eventually came to a solution. They told me that they had taught me well and trusted that I would make the right decisions. If my grades didn't suffer and I didn't get into trouble, I could stay out later, but the moment I got into any trouble, I wouldn't be able to DJ anymore and my curfew would be 10:00 P.M. That way I controlled my own fate. I don't know what made them choose this approach, but it was perfect for me. I won't say I never did anything I shouldn't have, but this gave me an incentive to stay out of trouble and taught me the importance of personal responsibility. Because of this, I always knew where to draw the line.

Like many people my age, I grew up watching a considerable amount of TV. Many of the characters became American icons. As a Black child growing up in Gary, Indiana, I watched whatever predominately-Black shows were available; however, I also watched the same shows that mainstream America watched, and so did all the other Black kids. This was so engrained in the fabric of our day-to-day lives that it went unnoticed. There was clearly nothing unusual about it.

When I was little, I watched TV shows such as *Three's Company*, *The Dukes of Hazard*, *The Brady Bunch*, etc. and my mom never seemed to bat an eye. Then, in 1984, *The Cosby Show* debuted. It was like nothing that had ever been seen on TV before. Previously, all of the shows with Black casts were up-from-nothing stories, were slapstick, or were played to the benevolence of Whites. *The Cosby Show* was a story of a happily-married professional Black couple with decent kids. More importantly, it was done well and was funny. It was a tremendous hit. From that day forward, my mom wouldn't watch a show unless it starred Black actors. I would suggest a new show she might like. When I asked her what she thought, she would say that she didn't see any Blacks so she'd stopped watching. I call it the 'Cosby Show effect'.

I had grown accustomed to questioning everything and felt that my opinions were consistent with everything I had learned up to this point; however, I started to notice that they were very different from what other Blacks believed. What surprised me most was learning that my mother's beliefs seemed different from what I'd learned from her while I was growing up. It seemed that her opinions, like that of most of the people I spoke to, used emotion, racism, selfishness, or stereotypes to defend their arguments. I was naïve enough to use logic. So, this leads me back to television.

After *The Cosby Show* had been on for a couple of years, I was quite intrigued by the positions people took over its success. It became so much more than just a television show. Some Whites argued that the show was inaccurate. There was no way, in their minds, that a Black family could really be headed by two professionals. Though obviously not the norm, it is common for professionals to date and marry other professionals, making the premise quite logical. At the same time, many Blacks thought its success meant that half of the upcoming new shows would be based on Black characters.

As we progressed through the 1990s and started to deal with 'Post Cosby TV', lots of new shows starring Blacks were, in fact, launched. This was enhanced greatly by the creation of the WB and UPN networks. By the end of the decade, 59 shows with predominately-Black casts had been launched, however, only a handful stayed on the air longer than one season.[2] Many people in the Black community blamed the failure of these shows on racism and continued to say that Blacks were underrepresented on TV. While these accusations can't be completely dismissed, many factors could have contributed to this.

First, we have to admit that *The Cosby Show* was done extremely well and drew in a diverse audience. That being said, it allowed shows that would never have been launched to get a chance. If one of these new shows had anywhere near the success of *The Cosby Show*, it would not have been canceled. Green is more powerful than Black and White, as evidenced by the large number of predominately Black shows that were aired in the next decade. The second thing we must admit is that many of the 'Post Cosby TV' shows weren't very good. It was no different than any other year when the networks air a bunch of shows trying to see what will stick, but most of them get canceled. This happens every year to a great number of shows. Race cannot be completely dismissed as a factor in programming choices, but the same could be said for the number of shows that Blacks felt were needed to achieve adequate representation of the

17

Black community. It always seemed that 'more' was the only thing that could have satisfied them. I heard some Blacks say they felt that half of the shows on TV should be predominately Black. This didn't seem logical. This brings me to the two points I made that brought ire from my friends and family.

In 1996, Jesse Jackson organized a boycott of the Academy Awards.[3] He drew criticism from some Blacks because he picked the year Quincy Jones was producing and Whoopi Goldberg was hosting to boycott the show. Let me be clear that I disagreed with his boycott, but in his defense, he was boycotting the lack of Black nominees, so the host and producer of the show being Black had nothing to do with his argument. My logical observation was aimed at the boycott itself and the complaints of programming on TV, but it really goes to the core of why I see things differently and why it's so hard to make great strides in race relations.

Blacks were demanding more TV shows featuring Blacks, and Jesse was boycotting the Academy Awards, demanding more Black nominations, but what about other races? I always thought it was odd that when people talk about race they generally say Black and White. It seemed obvious to me that eliminating other races from the conversation stymied racial progress. What about Asian-Americans, Hispanics, Native Americans, etc.?

By the mid-nineties, there had been only two predominately Asian-American shows, one predominately Hispanic show, and none that represented any other minority groups. All but *Chico and the Man* were canceled after their first season, and all of the shows were comedies. I could not understand how people talked about equality and fairness but totally neglected a large portion of the population. If we truly wanted fair representation on TV, wouldn't we say something about the fact that, as of 2012, there have still only been two shows with predominately Asian-American casts? At least in the time since the mid-nineties, Hispanics have produced several shows. There have even been new networks developed for Hispanic audiences, but where's the progress for Asian Americans? Pat Morita had a show in 1976.[4] Margaret Cho had a show eighteen years later in 1994.[5] It's been another eighteen years, so aren't we due for another Asian American show? Logically, if programming was based solely on the demographics of the population, there would be at least some shows representing every race, several representing Asian Americans, and Hispanics would have more shows than Blacks. Here is a breakdown of the U.S. populations by Race/Ethnicity as of 2010.[6] As you can see, the Hispanic population outnumbers that of Blacks. Hmm... perhaps Jackson's boycott was warranted but just represented the wrong group.

Race / Ethnicity	% of U.S. population
White	63.70%
Hispanic or Latino	16.30%
Black or African American	12.20%
Asian	4.80%
Two or more races	1.90%
American Indian or Alaska Native	0.70%
Some other race	0.20%
Native Hawaiian or other Pacific Islander	0.20%

Another observation that got me into trouble was my response to people saying that Blacks aren't represented as often on TV anymore. This came in the early 2000s, after many of the new shows were canceled and were not replaced with predominately Black shows. My argument, which was unpopular with my friends, was that if you want to have a true representation of society, having TV shows with predominately Black casts was not the answer. I thought that the subtle change I saw in network TV made more sense to me than adding more predominately Black shows. What was happening, and what most of my friends didn't notice, was that TV shows started to become a better reflection of society.

Instead of Black shows and White shows, there were shows with diverse casts. Now, it was okay for White characters to have Black friends, neighbors, and bosses. It was slowly becoming more like reality. Even though many people still lived in segregated neighborhoods, they were still forced to interact with many different people. It was time for TV to make this leap as well. I was a big fan of Seinfeld, which was another show my mom said was racist because it had no Blacks. I actually thought it was one of the best representations of the real world. No, it didn't have a Black primary character, but how many Jewish men in their mid-thirties had close Black friends in the early '90s? Okay, Jerry's real life friendship with comedian George Wallace is an exception. So they brought the diversity of America into our homes in the best way possible — creative situations with everyday New Yorkers. Again, my logical argument was shot down. I was wrong, not because it didn't make sense, but because it kept Blacks from having more leading roles. After several attempts at convincing the Black people who I knew that this was the best way to get a true representation of our society, I realized they didn't want a true representation of our society; they wanted more predominately Black shows.

Up to now, I have used the subjects of music and TV to illustrate the effects that emotional thinking has on how we act. When this approach is taken with serious subjects, the results can be detrimental and long lasting. Let me also say that I am not implying that Blacks are the only group who use this line of thinking, nor are they more inclined to act in this manner than any other group. My observations were based on the environment I grew up in, so my scope was limited; however, I also believe that while other groups share this emotional thinking, it is most detrimental to the Black community. As I broadened my exposure, I learned not only how prevalent this approach was but how it leads to baseless assumptions and prejudices.

Differences, Stereotypes, and Assumptions

When I was in high school, I went to visit my older brother who was a student at Purdue University. That visit opened my eyes to just how sheltered my life was in Gary. Although I didn't get fully immersed in the college culture, some differences were evident. The first thing I noticed was the music. It was the music I had been introduced to years earlier by my friend's uncle. All through high school, I listened to that music under a shroud of secrecy, and now it was everywhere. Parties, restaurants, sporting events — everywhere I went — the air was filled with Def Leppard, Foreigner, Poison, and Van Halen. My next big eye opener was the diversity. Having come from a city where, aside from an occasional teacher or store owner, everyone was Black, this was fascinating. I am pretty sure that, at 17 years old, this was the first time I had seen an Asian-American. Though I was being exposed to a lot that I hadn't seen before, there was one thing I noticed that confused me. I noticed that people seemed to travel in groups. I didn't understand it, but I wasn't there long enough to really observe it. That was about to change.

At the end of the following school year, I started college at Indiana University. When I got there, I was impressed with how alluring and vast the campus was. Although I had spent the previous summer visiting my brother at Purdue, the makeup at Indiana University seemed different. The campus seemed to be more alive and charming than the Purdue campus. There was also a big difference in the demographics. Indiana University had a highly-respected school of music that rivaled Julliard. This brought in a diverse group of students from all over the world.

As I got settled in, I got to know several of the guys on my floor. Once classes started, I got a greater education in the types of groups people formed, which were similar to what I'd noticed while visiting my brother in Purdue, but now I had time to observe and try to understand. It seemed that these groups were formed by many alliances. They were grouped by, but not limited to; race, major of study, religion, sex, and national origin, and they all remained separate from each other. The Blacks were separate from the Whites, while fraternity and sorority students were separate from non-affiliated students, and the rich students were separate from the students lacking means. It seemed odd to me. Was this how the entire society was segmented?

This never stood out more than during meals. The cafeteria was like a gangland war zone. Everyone sat in their groups, and you were called on it when you didn't. I remember a Black kid going to lunch with one of his White friends. A group of us came in together, and they noticed him sitting there. A couple of people at the table actually expected him to move. He did not. No one said anything then, but he did receive flack later for it.

24

Notice, I said, "A group of us came in together." Everyone was pretty much coerced into some group or another, and since I visibly fit in with them, I was relegated to dine with the other Black students. It wasn't as if I had a problem with them or didn't get along with them; it just seemed odd to me that it was assumed that these were the people with whom I should be hanging out. This had never been an issue for me before. When I was a kid, I hung out with whoever was around. In Dalhart, they were all White, in Gary, all Black. This was different. In those other situations, they were the only kids around. Here, at Indiana University, it was as if we were being assigned — and I had a problem with that. I thought that I should be the one to choose with whom I would hang out, based on similar interests or with whom I could get along. I also saw it as my first chance to develop a deeper understanding of the differences and similarities of other people. I didn't leave the inhibiting and limiting segregation found in Gary, Indiana to attend a predominately White university and be forced to avoid White people and hang out with Black students only.

All groups have similarities and differences. Some of these are innate, while some are based upon our environment and experiences. Some of these characteristics are small things that become a part of you but go mostly unnoticed, while others become a defining part of your being and dictate many of your day-to-day decisions. We all have both of these types of characteristics. These similarities and differences dictate who we marry, who our friends are, where we live, and where we work. They have such a profound effect on who we are, yet we never think about why we feel the way we do or whether we're right or wrong. In most cases there is no right or wrong, and having these characteristics can help strengthen who you are while having no effect on others. However, many problems arise when people assume to know what others' beliefs are or when they try to force their beliefs on others in an attempt to change them.

As time went on, I started to see how the different groups, especial racially divided ones, related to one another. The stereotypes, the closed-minded behavior, and the prejudices I observed shocked me. When I was younger and around the White kids, race wasn't an issue because we were so young, back in Gary, it wasn't an issue because we were all the same race. Now, in the midst of all of this diversity, everything was kept so segregated. However, initially, the negativity was muted. I did not see any overt acts of prejudice. There would be looks or muffled comments, but nothing I could easily pinpoint. As I got to know the other kids, things slowly started to come out. I would hear about Black students being treated poorly and about places I shouldn't go because of racists. I also heard many of the Black students making mean generalizations about Whites. Some were based on things they had seen, but others on innuendo and prejudice. The problem is, they were taking things that could apply to anyone regardless of race and attributing them to all White people. Ironically, these were the same types of generalizations that we abhor being used toward Blacks.

Then, for the first time, I saw the other side of this. I had befriended some White students whom I had met in various classes and in my dorm. We got along just fine, yet when it came time to hang out or go to an event or party, they would always go with their White friends. Once, I left a class on the other side of campus and wanted to get lunch. A girl in the class was going the same way, so we decided to go to lunch together. We received some of the dirtiest looks I had ever seen. People assumed we were dating and openly disapproved, solely because she was White and I was Black. As we were leaving, two White girls passed us on their way into the cafeteria. They turned to her and said, "What are you doing with *him*?" Not only did I think it was bold for them to say something, but I found it interesting that they addressed their comments directly to her. Their selfishness led them to take it as a personal affront that my White classmate would be seen out with me even though they did not know either of us. This dynamic of race relations didn't really sink in until I saw it applied by people who I knew.

As can be the case in high school, college is difficult socially when you don't fit in. I never had much of an issue with this. Since I never fully identified with any specific group, I never got fully associated with one. Outside of being automatically aligned with the other Black students, I remained fairly independent. I did see other students who struggled with fitting in. I remember one such student, who was Black, who seemed like a nice person. He was never accepted by any of the 'groups' and most people thought he was a little strange. I remember him trying to get to know several of the Black girls in our dorm. They shot him down viciously, which made the reaction I later saw them exhibit that much more memorable.

A couple of weeks after he had unsuccessfully asked these girls out, we were in the cafeteria having lunch and sitting at the 'Black' table as usual. In walked the strange student who no one wanted to hang out with, and he was accompanied by a White girl. They sat at a table on the other side of the room, and it didn't take

27

long before they became the topic of conversation. The girls at our table, several of whom had shot him down just weeks earlier, called the attention of everyone at the table to the couple. They proceeded to speculate, aloud, about what these two were doing together. A couple of the guys started laughing and asked why they cared. One of the girls said, "Those White girls are always stealing our men. Besides, he probably thinks he's special because he's with that White girl."

I told these Black girls that I had seen him ask them out and that they had all said no. I asked them what they thought he was supposed to do. They didn't respond, but we had to keep them from confronting him. Again, they didn't let the fact that this had nothing to do with them stop them from selfishly making it about themselves.

One interesting product of the diversity of the campus was how it sometimes forced different groups to interact. Although people gravitated to social groups with whom they felt most comfortable, it didn't eliminate other groups from forming out of necessity or proximity. Students had study groups, athletic groups, etc. But the greatest forced groups were formed in the dorms. Some students had friends who attended school with them, so they requested their roommates, but many of us were paired with random students. For the Black students, this meant that most of us had White roommates. Regardless of their differences, many of these paired roommates got along — even the ones who didn't tried to be cordial. This led to a series of open discussions about race.

These discussions addressed stereotypes and were designed to help increase understanding amongst the races. There would be a small group of students of mixed races and backgrounds and they were free to ask anything they wanted. They asked about hair, food, cleanliness, language, physical attributes, and many other topics typically considered taboo. Occasionally arguments would ensue, but overall there were very few incidents. Many still held their beliefs in the stereotypes, but it was interesting to hear the discussion. Some of the things that were said were loosely based on facts, and most of them were completely fabricated. Whichever category they fell into, I found it hard to believe that anyone could actually think that these stereotypes accurately described every Black or White person. Not only did they believe many of the stereotypes, but most of them didn't even know where they had gotten them. In some cases they had heard these things from their parents, but this seemed to be a small percentage. For most of us it was just out there, hushed conversations from adults, TV, movies, and popular music all alluded to these common stereotypes. Even classic books we read in school made mention of them. Over time, they slowly get into your subconscious and you start to take it as fact. I must admit that I cannot recall ever hearing my parents use any of these stereotypes, yet most of them I had heard. Although I believed most of them to be untrue, even the ones that I thought a group had a propensity toward, I could not logically assume that it fit all or even most of that group. I would soon see that others felt differently.

After these conversations, some of the Black students would get together and talk about the topics that were discussed. I imagine that the White students did the same thing. The biggest thing I learned from all of this was how divided the races were. What was most telling was the fact that they were able to use logic to dispel negative stereotypes about their own group while maintaining a belief in stereotypes about other groups that didn't logically make sense. From these discussions amongst the Black students, my logical way of thinking led me to another realization. When some of the Black students discussed how they had come to believe certain stereotypes about Whites, they described things they had been taught, secondhand accounts of things that had happened to someone they knew, and their own experiences. As I stated earlier, we base most of our beliefs on these things. Most of the Black students came from all-Black communities, as did I, but unlike me, they didn't have other diverse experiences to balance this out. If all they had were negative experiences with Whites, then why would they think any differently? Then, logically speaking, this works for other groups as well.

Like the Black students, most White students grew up in homogeneous neighborhoods. And like our parents, most of their parents were not overtly racist and didn't teach them to embrace stereotypes, but they probably didn't dispel them either. I'm sure most of the White students didn't grow up with many Blacks in their neighborhood, and if they did, they didn't go out of their way to make friends with them. So, with that said, why didn't any of the students consider that if most of the perceptions and stereotypes existing about their group were untrue, that premise would hold true for other groups as well? If, for instance, as a Black person you know that not every Black person is a violent, uneducated criminal, and you think it is foolish and dangerous to believe that, wouldn't it also be foolish and dangerous to believe that stereotypes you hear about White people are true about every White person? Logic makes this easy to understand, but, unfortunately, in most cases we do not use logic to form our opinions and judgments of people. I have noticed that along with stereotypes and assumptions, selfishness plays a big part in how we perceive things and has a powerful influence on how we form our opinions.

The Impact of Stereotypes and Selfishness

In many of the debates I had, I noticed an underlying trait present in many of the opposing positions. I began to understand that we could not come to an agreement, but it was not because we didn't want the same results but because we were not basing the argument on the same information. I was taking the information available and using logic to determine my position. They were taking their desired outcome and crafting the information to fit that outcome. This brought me to one simple realization: People are selfish. Most of us possess some level of selfishness in our character. Some will say it is inherent. It is normal for people to have their best interest at heart. This isn't necessarily a bad thing — when it's not in excess. However, this can skew the way we see things.

For example, selfishness played a large part in the Academy Award boycott as well as the complaints about TV programming I mentioned earlier. Do you think that if the executives for all of the major TV networks got together and vowed to make 12% of all programming predominately Black going forward, a fair representation of the population, that the Blacks who were complaining would be satisfied? We can never be sure, but I would venture to say no. The worst impact that selfishness has is when it causes us to take something that has nothing to do with us and creates an imaginary effect on us. In my story about the Black guy who came into the lunchroom at college with the White girl, this is what the girls at our table did. They reacted as if his sitting with the White girl was a slight on them. They assumed that it made the statement that the White girl was better than they were. This was an illogical conclusion, since he had asked a couple of them out first and they had turned him down. Selfishness can be bad when it causes us to want more than our fair share or want something that isn't ours. It can also lead to us being jealous of others.

We know that most stereotypes are untrue, but there are several reasons why they are so hard to combat. First, there are the stereotypes that people think are positive. For example, we have all heard that Blacks are good dancers or better at basketball. Being Black has nothing to do with a person's ability to do either of these things, but since it's not a negative stereotype, Blacks take ownership of it. They begin to accept it, subconsciously, as truth. Ironically, it doesn't make them instantly believe they can dance or play basketball; the mind wouldn't comprehend that. What it does is create the fallacy that the opposite must be true.

Have you ever heard a person say, "He's a good basketball player — for a White guy?" There's no logic behind it, but the pride obtained from being able to own those inherent skills makes it a surprise when a Black person sees a talented White basketball player. The same goes for White singers supposedly having 'soul'. Again, it's as if Blacks have ownership of being the soulful singers. When the stereotype isn't negative, those who are members of that

34

group are less likely to protest. Asians are good at math; Jewish people are good with money; men are good at fixing things; Mexicans are hard working. We've all heard statements such as these, and they are usually not followed by someone saying, "Hey, that's racist!" or a member of that group being offended and starting a fight. Although they know these statements aren't factual, many people in these groups take a little pride in having something positive associated with them. However, no stereotype is harmless; even those that sound positive can have a negative effect on some members of the group being prejudged and on society as a whole.

For instance, an Asian student may feel pressured to excel at math because of the stereotype regarding Asians' assumed superlative abilities in mathematics. Men often feel pressured to try to fix things they know nothing about to avoid the anxiety of having to admit they are not handy. Now, consider the other side. How would you feel if you were one of the final two candidates for a job and you had similar experience as the other candidate, but the hiring manager chose the other person because he or she was Jewish and therefore better with money? On the other hand, maybe the job entails long hours and the other candidate is picked because he or she is Mexican and therefore will work harder. In these situations, the stereotypes are not so harmless.

As you can see, even the stereotypes that many consider to be positive have negative influences on us. The biggest problem with overcoming stereotypes is, although they are not true, we think that there are facts to support them. But like all statistics, you need to look at all of the information. Since most of us never actually look at any data, we tend to go on memory. Therefore, if we hear a stereotype and then constantly hear stories and see examples that it is true, it becomes a reality in our minds and it changes how we react when faced with those being stereotyped. The best, and by that I mean the 'worst', example of this is the belief that Black men are violent criminals who need to be avoided.

We've all heard the statistics: Blacks are 38% of the inmates and 13% of the population, compared to Whites who are 32% of the inmates but over 65% of the population.[7] Additionally, blacks are imprisoned at six times the rate of Whites (based on 2010 numbers). These are alarming stats and are unfortunately true. Although this problem has many contributing factors that need to be addressed, these numbers have a dramatically negative effect on Blacks, and they unfairly contribute to the stereotype. Politicians and some in the media use these statistics to create news stories and point out things on which officials can focus; however, these statistics also create an unfair bias against Blacks — Black men specifically. Constantly sharing these numbers without the balance of the data causes many Black men undue police targeting, negative assumptions, and, in some cases, violent overreactions. I have had White people ask me why Blacks are so violent. Some suggested that we are simply more violent than other races and mention these statistics. The following stat is a better indication of crime rates. Here are the incarceration rates for the entire population by race:

Whites – .25%
Blacks – 1.6%
Hispanics – .69%

While stating that the rate for Blacks is six times that of Whites is true, less than 2% of the Black population is a far cry from the assumption that most Blacks are out committing crimes and therefore you should be afraid. You must also keep in mind that most of the crimes committed by Blacks happen in Black neighborhoods, which drastically diminishes the impact on the entire population.

Finally, to address the notion that we are innately more violent, if you adjust for socio-economic issues, such as income, education, unemployment level, and family history, one could argue that it brings the numbers down to an equal level. My point here is that although the violence in the Black community is higher than in other communities, there is no valid basis to believe that Blacks are more violent than any other group, and, more importantly, it proves that like all other stereotypes this is not based on fact. Most of the views Whites have of Blacks are based on the crime about which they constantly hear. Also, all the years of Blacks being portrayed in TV and films as slaves, servants, and criminals has been engrained in the psyche of America.[8] These things *have* to affect the way Blacks are portrayed by others. Here are a couple of examples.

A friend told me a story about an observation he had. Without any knowledge of my writing, he told me about an impromptu study he began. He catches the train into the city for work. As anyone who commutes to a large city can tell you, people pack the trains and buses like sardines and will often knock someone down just to get a seat. One morning he got on the train as usual and took a seat. Several other people got on as well, but he didn't really notice them. At the next stop, he noticed that a young Black man who had gotten on at the same time he did had an empty seat next to him, and for a second he thought people were avoiding it. He found this interesting, so he started paying closer attention. When the train pulled into the next station, he could see people going through the thought process to decide where to go. Some went toward the front of the car, some toward the back, and others just remained standing. None of them sat next to the Black man. As the train made its subsequent stops, he saw a couple of people make a motion as if they were going to take the seat, but then they changed their minds. Finally, after several stops, and only when there were no seats left, someone took the seat. My friend had never noticed this before and thought it was just a coincidence. But, of course, he had never watched for it either.

When he told me this, he mentioned that he was considering doing a study to see what the results would be. I thought it was a great idea and decided to do it myself. I would monitor the same scenario on my commute to work for an entire week to see how often it happened. I know there could have been any number of reasons why people didn't take the seat — preference to front or rear of the car, preference of window or aisle, the cleanliness of the seat, number of stops, etc. so, after three days of watching, I felt I needed to increase the study to get a better sample. I realized the scenario couldn't be manipulated, so I decided to monitor the train for two weeks. There had to be a Black person with an open seat next to him, which wasn't the case on every trip, and there was no way to account for another Black person getting on at the next stop and taking the seat. After two weeks of watching, I got the same results as my friend. In cases where the desired scenario was achieved, people skipped the seat next to the Black person for several stops. The seats were taken quicker if it was a Black woman or an older Black man, but only after most of the other seats were taken. I also noticed that in several of the instances, people would get up and take another seat if they were seated next to a Black person and someone in another seat got off the train. I began to wonder if other people noticed this. While this is not a scientific study and simply one man's findings from a brief observation, it does help us understand how prejudices and stereotypes are so strong and so prevalent that they have become part of the subconscious of many people.

This is similar to what author Malcolm Gladwell pointed out in *Blink*. He took the Race Implicit Association Test[9] given by Harvard and was shocked by the results. Before the test is administered, you are asked what your attitudes toward blacks and whites are. Then the test starts. You are shown a series of pictures and asked to associate certain words with the pictures. Gladwell took the test four times yet the results were unchanged. In describing the consistency of the results, Gladwell said, "It turns out that more than eighty percent of all those who have ever taken the test end up having pro-White associations, meaning that it takes them measurably longer to complete answers when they are required to put good words into the 'Black' category than when they are required to link bad with Black people."[10] He was found to have a moderate automatic preference for whites and went on to say, "The IAT . . . can be a powerful predictor of how we act in certain kinds of spontaneous situations."[11] These subconscious beliefs may have affected the way the people behaved who my friend and I watched on the train.

Another example of how prejudice shapes our views on race is a recent news story about an altercation in the Wrigleyville neighborhood in Chicago. This summer, a group of men went out to shoot a music video. They borrowed a friend's limo and went up to the Wrigleyville area where there are plenty of bars and people hanging out. Around 3:00 A.M., an altercation occurred between the men in the limo and some people from the neighborhood. When the story hit the news, there were varying descriptions of what had happened.[12] What I found is that the opinion of the story became more interesting than the story itself.

This was the topic on a local talk radio show on the Monday after the event. There were two on-air personalities debating their opinions. One said that the men in the limo were animals being violent for no reason, and the other said that we don't know what happened. After a few minutes of back and forth they opened the phone lines. Some callers agreed with one personality and some with the other. The response was no different than a typical debate until a man called who was upset about the coverage of the story.

He was upset because neither the TV anchors nor the personalities on the radio had mentioned the race of the accused or the victims. One of the personalities then mentioned that the guys in the limo were Black and the victims were White, but she said she didn't see how that mattered. The caller said he knew the racial details and wondered why they wouldn't say it. After him, they got a stream of calls involving race. One caller said, "That's how they are." Another said, "They're all violent." One woman said she is nervous around them and usually tries to avoid them. At this point, the personality who had said they were animals said, "When did this become about race?" She said that when she had said they were animals, she was talking about that specific group of men in the limo and the way they behaved. She went on to say that it was irrational to make blanket statements about an entire race based on one incident. Can't we though? It didn't take long to get there.

We may never know what actually happened that night. Based on what we do know, it's hard to side with the guys in the limo, but that's still based on assumption. It just seems logical that if they were being harassed or people were yelling things at them, all they had to do was drive away. That being said, how do their actions make me, a Black man, also a violent person? When those callers heard the story and made those comments, that is what they said. All their 'they' and 'them' statements were aimed directly at me and millions of Black men like me who had nothing to do with the incident. Talk about sweeping statements.

These are just a couple of examples of how Whites' stereotypes about Blacks affect their behavior. However, Whites are not the only ones who have developed in their subconscious negative attitudes about Blacks. I also believe that for an unfortunate number of Blacks, the constant visual of negative and violent images along with constant exposure to stereotypes and prejudice through the years has had an effect on how they view themselves as well.

It is obvious that music has had a dramatic influence on my life. When I was younger, the Parents Music Resource Center was formed in an attempt to censor some music they deemed explicit.[13] I still remember their 'Filthy Fifteen' list. At the time, I was vehemently opposed to all forms of censorship. My belief was that you should be able to express yourself as you pleased, and if you didn't like it then you shouldn't buy it. I further thought that it was the parents' job to monitor what their children did. This was one of the reasons I later refused to vote for Al Gore; however, I must admit that as a teen I overlooked the fact that many children did not have the positive influence of a responsible adult. When I was in high school, not only did I listen to many of the songs on the 'Filthy Fifteen' list, but I also listened to NWA, the 2 Live Crew, and many others whom Tipper and Co. would have deemed inappropriate. However, these things were offset with other media and the positive values that had already been instilled.

Throughout the years, teens have always rebelled, and there has always been some level of negative media out there. But things have advanced so quickly that parental controls have not been able to keep up. Thirty years ago, there were limited cable stations and no Internet. Now, you can see and hear what you want twenty-four hours a day. I have to concede that if you were to listen to "How I Can Just Kill a Man" and play Grand Theft Auto all day, it would eventually have a negative effect on your psyche and desensitize you to violence. That being said, the recent onslaught of violent and misogynistic stimuli knows no color and has not been limited to just Black men. In addition, exposure to this type of stimulus alone would have a negative effect on someone. It would have to be a perfect storm combining the right set of living circumstances, mental state, and perhaps predisposition to these negative behaviors with the constant exposure to the triggering stimuli. Still, what is most disturbing is that much of the negative stereotypes about Blacks in the media come from Black artists. The songs, TV shows, and films created by Blacks do little to improve the perceptions of Blacks, and in many cases, it adds to the existing negative ones.

42

Most of us are honest and caring people, and we believe that life is sacred and that its value cannot be measured. We say that all lives are equal, but we don't necessarily react in this way. We have more concern for a family member than we do for a stranger and more sympathy for a sick child than for a person we deem evil, such as a murderer or a rapist. We care about anyone who suffers and we sympathize with them; however, there are details about a story that add to or detract from the level of sympathy or interest we have with a story. When we hear the news, and some detail about the story touches us personally, we tend to pay closer attention.

For instance, when we hear a story about a robbery, we tend not to pay close attention because we're inundated with so many of these stories. Once the newscaster says the victim was an elderly person, we pay closer attention. On some level, we feel that it's worse to rob an older person than a younger person. How about a story concerning a person with a rare disease, where our level of sympathy increases if we find out that it's a child. These are common reactions, but there are several other details a little more specific to a person's individual beliefs. This is part of our selfish nature and our innate desire for self-preservation. Religion, race, and sex, and other specialized details, also play a part in the level of interest in the story. This is why Blacks see a story about a crime and say to themselves, and sometimes aloud, "Please don't let the offender be Black!" These are the details that are often driven by stereotypes and prejudices, and I'd like to explore these.

Since the implementation of the Amber Alert,[14] there has been greater coverage of child abductions. However, news teams across the country seem to put greater focus on the stories where White children have been abducted or abused than they do children of other races.[15] It is difficult to gauge since you can't measure what you don't know, and since there was no coverage of some lesser-known cases, many of us don't know there were other abductions or abuses to cover. But let's assume there are abductions that are not getting coverage; why aren't they? Is it because the people who choose the stories that are aired or printed are racist? We definitely cannot rule that out, but like the earlier situations with the predominately Black shows, TV executives' first priority is ratings. We have to assume they'd air it if it got ratings. This begs the question: Do people have more sympathy for and therefore more interest in a story based on the race of the people involved? The simple answer is yes. This is not to say that people think a White child's life is more valuable than a Black child's life, though some do. At its most basic level, this goes back to the selfishness in all of us. While selfishness can be a strong factor, there are times when race also plays a part.

Unfortunately, 2012 has been a terrible year for gun violence. Whether it's senseless mass shootings, Florida's 'Stand your ground' law, or gun crimes in urban areas, the violence has been all too frequent. Every time one of these stories makes national news, the debate on gun control is revisited. For the purposes of this book, where you stand on this issue doesn't matter. What's important is how the stories are approached. Let's look at two of the most memorable stories of the year: the Trayvon Martin shooting and the attack at the Aurora, Colorado movie theater.

On February 26, 2012, George Zimmerman, a self-appointed neighborhood watchman, shot and killed Trayvon Martin. The 17-year-old Martin was unarmed and returning to his father's home from the store.[16] Zimmerman was questioned and released. He claimed self-defense, while many thought the shooting was racially motivated. Black journalists and activists pushed to get mainstream media coverage and demanded Zimmerman's arrest. There were protests, celebrities spoke out, and Al Sharpton went to Florida demanding justice.[17] The Miami Heat Basketball Team even wore hoodies.[18] Why was this case so compelling?

Race is the only logical reason there was this level of outrage. Clearly, the shooting of any unarmed person must be investigated, and I see nothing wrong with gun control proponents wanting a review of the 'Stand your ground' law; however, the fact that Trayvon was unarmed cannot be the only reason this got so much attention. Dozens of people are killed in this country every day, many of them unarmed. Are the protesters saying that Trayvon's life is more important than the countless others who have been killed? Where was Al Sharpton in these other cases? It seems like race can determine how much we care about a victim. But this works both ways.

On July 20, a gunman opened fire in a crowded movie theater in Aurora, Colorado at the premiere of the movie *Dark Knight Rises*.[19] Because of the actions of this mentally-ill killer, 12 lives were lost and 59 people were wounded. There was round-the-clock coverage for days. Due to the shocking display of evil, this was expected. However, one has to ask: Is there a racial component to the lack of coverage of the gun violence in Chicago?

On the same night of the Aurora shooting, there were three killed and 18 wounded from shootings in Chicago.[20] While it's completely logical that these shootings were overshadowed by the Aurora massacre, what about the lack of coverage throughout the

45

year? As I stated, 2012 has been a terrible year of gun violence throughout the country, but nowhere has this been more evident than in Chicago. Throughout the summer, Chicago had several weekends where more than 20 people were wounded by gunfire and several weekends with numbers over 30. And as of the end of October 2012, there have been 436 people shot to death this year in Chicago, not including the countless number of injuries.[21] Is the reason there is so little coverage of the Chicago shootings because many of the faces of the victims are Black?

Some will say that much of the murder rate is due to gang violence, and people are less inclined to empathize with the victims. This may be the case, but many innocent victims have been caught in the crossfire. On June 27, 7-year-old Heaven Sutton was killed in such a shooting.[22] After being mentioned on that night's news, the only coverage this story got was when Mayor Rahm Emmanuel made his emotional but illogical plea to gang members saying, "We've got two gangbangers, one standing next to a kid. Get away from that kid. Take your stuff away to the alley."[23] Why is the fact that Chicago averages 1.5 people killed by gun violence every day not seen as a major problem? Race and socioeconomic status plays a large part.

This is not to say that the people on either side are racists. It would be unfair and shortsighted to say that every Black person who demands justice for Trayvon is a racist, as it would be unfair to say that every White journalist who reported on the Aurora massacre but said nothing about gun violence in Chicago is a racist. Yet we cannot ignore the fact that the excessive gun violence in Chicago didn't warrant a visit from Sharpton like Trayvon's shooting did and over 30 people being shot week in and week out in Chicago

46

didn't get continued coverage on CNN and Fox News. In fact, Bill O'Reilly is the only national TV anchor who continually covered the Chicago gun violence.

Whether it's a missing child or victims of gun violence, there's no doubt that race and our selfishness play a role in how the story is covered and how we react to it. This is a common reaction for many, and we can't change it if people cannot be honest about their feelings without being attacked or called a racist. If people could openly say, "I'm not racist; I just put my self-preservation first," then that would go a long way toward openness. Not everything is based in racism, and we often overlook the fact that Whites aren't the only ones who have these reactions. Let's put it this way: Most Blacks would say that if the child in the story was Black, then they would sympathize a little more than if the child was White. Sometimes selfishness trumps racism.

Let's say a news story comes on the TV warning about a series of rapes on a college campus. First, women listening to this story will pay a little more attention than men will. Then the story goes on to say that there have been four victims so far and that they were all 18-23 and White. What do you think Black women who attend this college are thinking? Are they racist? What about older students or professors? They are trying to put themselves at ease, and believing that they are not in the target group of the rapist gives them a level of comfort. This is why we are so deeply moved by senseless violence with seemingly no motive. Our compassion feels for the victims, and our subconscious is unable to make us safe by separating us from the victim's demographics. In situations where crimes are being committed, our selfishness causes us to pay closer attention

47

to the stories that may directly affect us and look for ways to convince ourselves that we're safe, but what about when safety isn't an issue? Do we use selfishness to make other decisions?

I was looking for charities in which to donate time and money. My wife sits on the board of directors for the Center for Abused Women And Their Children, an organization committed to ending domestic violence and providing shelter, counseling, and advocacy for women and children who are affected[24]. I wanted to dedicate time to an organization, and there are so many charities doing great work for people in need. I chose the Cara Program and started volunteering.[25] A few months later, I was talking to a couple of people and charity came up. One of them asked what types of services the charities I volunteered for provided. He mentioned that he wanted to find a charity he could volunteer with, and the other person asked if the charities I volunteer with were Black charities. I said no and was immediately scolded for not giving back to 'our' community. I thought it was a baseless attack, especially since neither of the people I was talking to volunteered at all, so I didn't bother to defend myself. It did make me wonder since I like to analyze things. What made someone who didn't volunteer time or money to any charity feel the need to disparage my benevolence? This led me to an even greater observation.

Since my wife and I both volunteer, we go to several fundraising events a year. We notice that there are very few Black people at these events. The same thing goes for the other volunteers we meet. So, my question is: Where are all the Black volunteers? Though these are not specific Black charities with Black or Negro in the name, over 70% of the people these charities help are Black, and regardless of race, I believe everyone has an obligation to give back. The amounts to give back vary based on what you can afford to give, but everyone who has something to give should do so.

After the initial charity conversation, I asked more of my friends about it and was surprised by how few of them donate money or time to any charities. I never really got a specific reason, but what I found is that many of them felt it was someone else's job to help people in need, usually the government. It struck me as odd, because as much as I hear Blacks say, "Whites don't care," Whites do the lion's share of donating beyond the discrepancy in populations and regardless of the race of those in need. I understand that their economic situation as a whole is much better than that of Blacks; however, that does not explain my friends and many other Blacks who can afford to give but don't.

Another area where selfishness and stereotypes are joined is when we generalize the actions and views of a certain group. People are grouped in many ways. They are grouped by gender, race, religion, income level, political party, etc. and based on these groupings, similarities are assumed to exist amongst its members. Grouping this way can be beneficial in some instances, but we tend to make assumptions about the entire group and proceed as if they are facts. There are two major flaws with these generalizations. First, not everyone in a given group will share the same view. Secondly, there will be situations when some members will belong to multiple groups. In these cases, how do you determine which group a person will side with when the views of the two groups vary?

For example, if we take a random sample of women, we may assume that they feel the same way about a topic that affects women, say, abortion. However, a percentage of those women sampled may break from the group. Due to other groupings, such as religion or marital status, they may feel they have beliefs that are the opposite of many women. Having one thing in common doesn't mean you agree on everything. So why should all Blacks agree that the Democratic Party is the right party for them? Also, what happens when a topic affects more than one of our core beliefs? How do we decide which belief takes priority?

Prior to Barack Obama becoming president, the Democratic nomination came down to Obama and Hilary Clinton. Most Blacks threw their support behind Obama, while many women supported Clinton. Both groups were excited about the idea of a major 'first'. However, what was expected of the Black woman voter? Was she a woman first or Black first? The decision was made more difficult by the fact that their views were similar. After Obama won the primary, what were the Black Republicans to do? Should they follow their beliefs or help make history? During the time leading up to the general election, I had several encounters that I found interesting. One particular instance was on the day before the election.

I was in line at a Starbuck's near my job when a young Black woman, having received her coffee and was turning to leave, walked in front of me to make her way to the door. As she passed me, she turned around and said, "We're going to win tomorrow." I may be in the extreme minority here, but I thought that was an odd thing for a random person to say to me, especially considering the setting and the fact that no one was having a conversation

50

about the election. Although the woman was clearly making an assumption about my political views, it was still harmless, but some assumptions aren't so harmless.

A co-worker and I were talking about the upcoming weekend. She mentioned that she was going to see the new Tyler Perry film. She told me she had heard him in an interview on the radio the previous day and that he was discussing how difficult it was to get his films made when, as she put it, silly crap like *Abraham Lincoln: Vampire Hunter* continues to be made. She went on to say that whenever a Black film comes out, she makes it a point to go see it even if she thinks it's going to be bad. I said I understand her wanting to support them, but as a consumer you vote with your dollar. If you continue to go to see stereotypical Black films that are poorly done, they're going to assume that's what you want to see and continue to make them.

She went on to say that her husband doesn't understand why she refuses to see certain films with certain actors. She said the same goes for sports. Her husband likes sports, but she won't watch many of the teams he likes because they have Black athletes who are married to White women. I asked her why she cared who someone she doesn't even know marries, and she said that she's just a little racist that way and she thinks everyone is. I told her that her views were selfish and illogical — but not racist. There's a distinct difference between the two. She told me she didn't like Dennis Rodman, Kobe Bryant, and other athletes, simply because they married other races. Conversely, she told me that she saw an athlete on *Dancing with the Stars* whom she is now a fan of because his wife is Black. She also said that she loves Robert DeNiro because he dates Black women. So,

51

not only does she want all *Black* men to marry Black women, she wants *everyone* to marry Black women. Talk about selfish! This was interesting to me, because it showed me truly how deep race preference and selfishness goes. This story is not that uncommon, although you may find it interesting to know that her husband is White.

Part II

RACISM

What is Racism?

"**J**ust because you're paranoid doesn't mean they're not after you!" This is a commonly heard phrase attributed to many sources from Joseph Heller to Kurt Cobain. I like to use a variation when speaking of racism, "Just because they call everything racism doesn't mean some of it isn't!" Though I've pointed out situations where race was not a factor or where minor assumptions may have been based on race but don't seem to have played a large part in the results, we cannot overlook the fact that racism still exists and has a profound effect on everyone who is exposed to it. The dictionary defines racism as, "A belief that race is the primary determinant of human traits and capacities and those racial differences produce an inherent superiority of a particular race."[26] This is a short and simple definition for something so powerful, yet very accurately stated. I've seen and heard definitions that vary slightly from this one, but they seem to be open for more interpretation. No one would argue whether racism exists, so I find it interesting that a conversation about racism can lead to such a debate. This debate is not about what we can do to combat or minimize racism; that I could understand.

Unfortunately, after so many years of exposure to it, we are still debating the most basic element of racism, what it is.

Although the dictionary definition is accurate, I've never heard anyone use it in discussions. So, what is it that most of us think racism is? Many people take the basic premise from the definition above and then add to it. This creates a flawed definition, which is illogical. The first error in logic people make in their definitions is stating that racism is the same as prejudice. The two are closely tied and often occur in similar situations, but you can have one without the other. We all make preconceived notions, yet we are not all racists. If, for example, a Black woman was walking down the street at night and saw a Black man, made a prejudicial assumption about him, and went into a store because she didn't feel safe, we wouldn't say she was racist. In this case, we would assume she was judging the situation and the person, but not *all* Black men. This could be the same if the woman was White, or perhaps she is racist, we just cannot know.

How about this: If a White man doesn't think Blacks are bad but he feels Whites are superior to Blacks, is he a racist? Though he may not have prejudice feelings about a Black person who he sees, the fact that he feels there is an innate superiority in Whites is racist. Another common mistake is that power or control is necessary to be a racist. This is a common fallacy amongst Blacks that allows them to believe that Blacks cannot be racists, but this is not factual. There are indeed situations where Blacks have control or power over others, but more importantly, control and power are not necessary elements of the presence of racism. Having power and control only adds to the effects of the racism.

56

In April of 2012, Jessica Elizabeth, a bartender at a club in Chicago, posted several racist comments on her Facebook page.[27] It made national news. At one point, her boss saw her posts and told her to take them down, but she continued. A local blogger copied the posts and made them public. She was subsequently fired. Most would agree that she's a racist. The fact that she had no power or control over anyone didn't make her comments any less offensive or prevent her from being a racist.

One belief I have is that there are varying levels of racism. Most people to whom I've mentioned this disagree with me, but here's my point: I'm not implying that everyone who says a race-based joke or believes a stereotype is racist. These jokes have been so ingrained in the fabric of our culture that it is impossible not to be aware of them, and it's understandable that we've all said one or two in our time. Earlier, I mentioned how stereotypes, assumptions, and selfishness all affect how we behave. These can lead to a mild form of racism. I believe there are three levels between which we need to differentiate.

Level one of racism is the mildest. The people at this level don't consciously have ill feelings toward other races. They may legitimately have friends of the race toward which their racism is directed. It's the initial reaction they will subconsciously have in certain situations. The earlier train experiment is an example of this. You have to call it racism, because race was the sole determinate of the decision. However, most don't believe themselves to be racist. The problem is that we can control our conscious mind but not our subconscious. They didn't realize they were reacting this way. I call it mild racism because it's involuntary. The result of the action was the same as overt racism, so it wouldn't be accurate to call it anything else.

Level two of racism is more overt but still not as blatant as level three. They are conscious acts based on race, but the perpetrator is more inclined to show a bias toward one race than any implied malice toward another. If, for example, a position was narrowed down to two equally qualified people, one Black and one White, with no qualities available to tip the scales in either candidate's favor, the manager chooses the White applicant. Yes, the White candidate was chosen based on race, but that was because they were equally qualified. If questioned, the hiring manager would tell you that if the Black person had been more qualified, the choice would have been different. In the manager's mind, there was no racial prejudice here. The final candidates were equally qualified, so a choice had to be made. Using race was not malicious. It's no different than using age, gender, marital status, etc. to make the decision, but keep in mind that using those criteria are also illegal. This, again, is racism, as it assumes an inherent superiority because of being White.

While the second level of racism is more severe than what I called mild racism, there is a clear difference between it and the third and final level. The people whose beliefs are at level three have a deep-seated hatred of a specific group. It may not be overt, since it is no longer acceptable in society, but they don't necessarily hide it. They are more likely to commit crimes against or openly show disgust toward a given race. It's the shocking hatred we associate with Germany in the 1930s and 1940s and with America from slavery through the late 1960s.

The evil that Jews and Blacks faced in these periods are among the most memorable. Though the openness of 'No Jews' signs or separate Black and White facilities is no longer tolerated, we still hear occasional stories reminding us that this type of hatred still exists. Every year or so we hear of a new story of blatant racism. Whether it's the gruesome dragging death of James Byrd, Jr. in Jasper, Texas[28], or the Mississippi couple who were denied their July 20, 2012 wedding in Crystal Springs, Mississippi because they were Black[29], we are continually reminded that this level of racism is out there. As much as I would like to believe that it's going away, I'm more inclined to believe that the people who feel this way have just learned to adjust their methods.

My first experience of this new method was in 1992. Kohl's Department Store was opening a new location in Northwest Indiana. They were taking applications for all positions, and my girlfriend and I decided to apply. She invited her friend to join us, and the three of us went to the storefront Kohl's had rented for the hiring event. As you would expect, there was a large crowd there, and after we filled out the applications, there was a line to turn them in to someone. We were excited to find out that they were doing a quick review of the applications as they received them. We noticed small groups throughout the store and speculated that it must be for different departments or positions. When my girlfriend and I got to the table, the person greeted us, said thank you, and told us someone would be contacting us if our experience fit their needs. While we waited for her friend, we watched her approach the table. The conversation lasted for about a minute or so, and she was escorted to one of the smaller groups. After about five minutes of waiting, I went up to the table where we had turned in our applications and asked about the other groups. The person we handed our applications to said

59

those were interviews being held for people who had applied earlier and had been called back. We were shocked! We knew this was a lie, because the three of us had come in together. What else could we assume was the reasoning? Her friend had the least experience of the three of us. We were all around the same age — one man and two women. We could only assume that race was a factor, she being the only White person in our group. As we looked around, there were no Blacks in any of the small groups, although there were many Blacks in line to apply. We left and vowed never to shop at Kohl's. I look back and realize it was the wrong response. I should have alerted the corporate office. It was unfair for me to assume that the entire company was racist because of the actions of one interviewer. It's possible that this person would have been removed, which could have given more Blacks a chance at employment. This is just another example of how we limit ourselves with our assumptions. I still have never set foot in a Kohl's.

Another sad but frequent reminder that this level of racism still exists can be found on the Internet. News stories often pop up on all the Internet home pages. When I see an interesting story, I read it and then scroll down to the most interesting part, the comment section. People are able to comment about whatever they want without real names or photos. In fact, besides character limitations and profanity, people will post just about anything. This anonymity has an interesting effect. It allows people to say what they really feel — things they wouldn't say if they had to identify themselves. It is here that you will see the most racist, inappropriate, illogical, and mean-spirited comments you've ever heard, all done under the cloak of secrecy.

One of the most memorable comments was following an article about the death of a former NBA player. I think this one stood out for me, because in many of the other stories I read, race, crime, or the economy was the topic, something that makes it easier to understand how a sick person can open the door to racist rhetoric. But in this case, there was nothing, no crime, nothing to debate. The story was about Armen Gilliam, a former NBA player who died at age 47 while playing basketball. Where he was from was mentioned, where he'd played college basketball, and how long he'd played in the NBA — that's about it. I read the article and then saw the post, "Great, one more dead nigger!" This reminds us that there are people out there who for no reason have an extreme level of hatred for others. The scariest part of this is that these are just ordinary people. We don't know who they are, where they live, or anything about them. We only know that they live among us and they hide their true identities when they walk away from their computers.

The third level of racism is what comes to mind when most of us think of racism. It is polarizing and in many cases dangerous. I like to think that the number of people who have this level of hatred has dwindled over the years, but how can I know for sure? You can't question them, and when pressed they won't admit it. I still believe that the war against racism can only be fought and won at levels one and two. First, though we cannot put a number on any level, I can all but guarantee that there are more people at levels one and two than at level three. And although it's obvious that those at level three are the worst, this in no way minimizes the actions of the other two levels. In fact, their actions may be harder to combat. One reason for this, as I've stated, is that there are simply more of them. Also, because those at level three are unapologetic, they are easier to identify. Those at levels one and two are more subtle and don't believe they have racist beliefs. This makes it harder to identify and harder to combat.

For instance, one phrase I've heard several times when meeting Whites at work or through friends was, "You're the Whitest Black guy I've ever met." This was clearly presented as a compliment. The point was that my clothing was normal, that I spoke clearly, and that my overall appearance and personality conformed to their ideas of a normal White American. Is this what the comment really says? According to them, I displayed a typical appearance and engaged in normal conversations. Why does that need to be complimented? What they were actually saying is that the norm for Blacks is to speak slang, to dress as if they're in a Rap music video, and not to be able to speak to Whites on their level. I was being complimented for raising myself above what in their eyes was the normal Black behavior. Isn't that racist? It clearly implies an inherent superiority of the White race. Worse yet, they did it in a way that allowed them to escape being called a racist. They can say, "See, I have Black friends." However, those friends aren't equal to their White friends; they are simply a few Blacks who they can tolerate because they are safe and don't resemble what they think of most Black people. It was actually just a selfish way to make them feel better about themselves. It didn't matter how they felt about most Blacks; having an occasional beer with me proved that they were not racist.

Lastly, we have what Bush called, "The soft bigotry of low expectations." He used this phrase to describe the situation of education in the country, focusing primarily on the discrepancy between rich and poor students. The "No Child Left Behind" initiative had many detractors. There's no way anything that big could be flawless, and I'm sure some of the detractors had valid points. Sticking strictly with the motives behind the arguments, it was interesting to hear people state that the goal of standardized testing was to limit minorities, with many stating that it was discriminatory. Were they saying that Black students weren't capable of learning certain things simply because they are Black? Or were they saying that being poor limits your ability to learn? If the person given the task to teach you thinks you can't learn the material, then how can you succeed? This is definitely an example of lowered expectations.

Looking back on my high school years, I am reminded that the teachers taught in only one speed, which did many students a disservice. Those who could not keep up were left behind with no real way to find help, while those who were more advanced were not challenged, which stifled their growth. Also, logic would say that if NCLB was racist for creating standards, isn't having failing schools with low standards in minority communities racist? Perhaps President Bush had a point. Either way, it's not the results that are always racist; sometimes it's simply the thought. This type of subtle racism is difficult to label. It is further complicated by the fact that the intentions are not known and the results are not Black and White.

Affirmative Action is one topic that usually starts a heated debate. My point is not to defend or disparage Affirmative Action but to be honest about its origin. No matter how you feel about it, can you say that if a White person is a proponent of Affirmative Action that he or she cannot be a racist? Some would say yes, but I say one has nothing to do with the other. My belief is that there are as many proponents of Affirmative Action that are racist as there are opponents, and we can't assume that those who oppose it do so because of racist beliefs. In many cases, the proponents are simply doing the opposite of the 'Whitest Black guy' compliment. Some proponents feel that Blacks are inferior and will not succeed without their help. While this helped many Blacks, and I think it would have been foolish to turn it down, especially in the 1960s and 1970s, we can't assume that it was done out of benevolence toward the Black community. Here's an example.

I was listening to a news program where they were discussing the Supreme Court's decision to hear the Affirmative Action case, Fisher v. University of Texas. This case involves a White student, Abigail Fisher, who claims that she was denied admission to the University of Texas while lesser-qualified Black applicants were accepted.[30] The guests on the program were debating the merits of the case and whether or not Affirmative Action is beneficial. One of the guests, a White attorney and former educator, argued for Affirmative Action. He said that he'd gone to public school in a majority White neighborhood and knew there was no way a Black kid from the inner city would have been able to compete with him or his classmates. He went on to say that an average student in his class would have tested better than the honor students from majority Black schools, so how can they succeed without Affirmative Action. The proponents of Affirmative Action on the show thought this was a great example for the need for the programs. I, on the other hand, thought the statement was clearly racist. He basically said that Whites were smarter and that you can't expect Blacks to succeed in a world with Whites without adjusting the course to account for their limited abilities. That is the very definition of superiority. How can that not be racist?

That being said, these are the reasons we have such a hard time agreeing on what racism is. It's not going be as obvious as the racist bartender's Facebook comments or the anonymous comments posted on the Internet. The problem we have in defining racism adds to the difficulty in properly identifying it or working to eliminate it. It may be overly optimistic, but I tend to believe there are far less racists in the country than my fellow Blacks believe. I compare it to the Whites' assumption of Black males being criminals or violent. Just as there are a small percentage of Black men who fit this, there is a small percentage of Whites who are racists, at least at the 2nd or 3rd levels described above. In both of these situations, the actions of those in the minority are unfairly attributed to the majority of each group.

We can't lump all three types of racism together or address them in the same manner. It is also illogical to assume that all of those who hold racist beliefs are Republicans while Democrats remain faultless. When taking an honest look at racism, there is another important factor we must discuss. What is the role Blacks have in America's racism?

The Role Blacks Play in Race Relations

There is no doubt that a percentage of the population is still driven by a racist agenda. My hope is that this number is dwindling. Those who carry these beliefs about others, however, can only change on their own. While Blacks have no blame in the racism of others, they do unwittingly contribute to the negative views some Whites have about the Black community, because many Blacks base their beliefs on misconceptions, are guided by selfishness, and don't use logic in their decision-making process. The combination of these three things creates a dilemma that often leads to poor judgment, bad actions, or exaggerated feelings of negativity. Earlier, I tried to dissuade people from thinking that power was the primary determinant as to whether or not a person is racist. It is obvious that up to this point my focus has been on White racism. However, it's important to admit that there is a segment of the Black population that is racist. It is a common theme in the Black community that Blacks cannot be racist. This is an obvious fallacy. Let's revisit the definition of racism. Are we saying that a Black person is not capable of believing that there are inherent differences between races and that their race is superior? Of course it's possible.

There needs to be a slight adjustment to the dictionary definition of racism. We should remove the part about superiority. One could argue that anyone who believes that race is the primary determinant of human traits and capabilities is racist regardless of whether or not they believe one race to be superior or not. With this as a guide, there is no way Blacks can be exempt from harboring racist views. In fact, you may be surprised to know that many Blacks believe that the majority of Whites are racist. It's not just that they believe racism still exists; most people believe that, but they believe that over 75% of all Whites are racist. This belief makes it easier for them to buy into stereotypes and is, in itself, racist.

Many Blacks are also guilty of some of the same racist beliefs Whites have about Blacks. Ask any Black person about the little talked about 'mixed company' reference, and, if honest, they will tell you it refers to the honest things they will say about Blacks to other Blacks but won't say in front of Whites. If Whites could be a fly on the wall in these conversations, they would hear talk that you wouldn't expect to hear about laziness, bad parenting, crime, and many other social problems. This is because they maintain a unified front and won't say in front of Whites what they truly believe and will say behind closed doors. However, Blacks are just as guilty as Whites are in maintaining the racial divide that exists today.

One thing that has always struck me as odd is the way Blacks view people of mixed races. Why do they feel they can dictate how a mixed-race person identifies himself or herself? For example, Mariah Carey is ½ Irish, ¼ Venezuelan, and ¼ Black, but when she identified herself as being multi-racial, many Blacks attacked her. Then there's Tiger Woods. In an interview on the Oprah Winfrey show, he called himself "Cablinasian", referring to his Caucasian, Black, American Indian, and Asian ethnicity. The Black community vilified him for years. When asked why they felt this way, the reason Blacks gave was illogical.

I was told that slave owners used to say that if you had a drop of Black blood in your veins, that made you Black. This belief was no doubt used so the children they produced by raping slaves remained as property. This was truly a vile, disgusting twist of logic for their advantage. So you see why I find it shocking that after all of the fighting and dying that Blacks have done for decades to combat racism, we've decided to buy into this opportunistic and racist belief.

If you notice, throughout this book, when addressing President Obama's race, I never refer to him as a Black man; it is always as non-White. I simply cannot understand how a child can come from the womb of a White woman, grow up estranged from his Black father while being raised by his White grandparents, and be seen only as Black. How can we triumph over racism when we can't even tell the truth as it is? I know I will be maligned more for this statement than anything else in this book, but sometimes I can't control my logical thinking.

The biggest area where stereotypes and selfishness affect the way racism is perceived is that it causes people to infuse race into situations that have nothing to do with race. This is something I call, "The Racism of Paranoia." As I've stated before, we are selfish by nature, and in many of these cases it's simply a matter of Blacks either feeling slighted or overlooked and blaming it on race. The problem is that these situations desensitize people to the racism that really exists. It can cause those who may otherwise sympathize with claims of racism to immediately question and sometimes doubt these claims. For every claim of racism that seems to be a stretch, there is a legitimate claim of racism where someone will say, "Here we go again." This is due to previous charges of racism they thought to be invalid.

There are also times, however, when the claim of racism doesn't even make sense. These are the most egregious because they add to the racial divide by making Blacks seem whiny and selfish to Whites while intensifying the belief that Whites are racists amongst Blacks who may believe the claim. Here are some examples of situations where race was unfairly made the focus.

When Charlize Theron announced that she had adopted her first child, many Blacks could be heard complaining about the fact that the child was Black. This stood out for me, because I'm sure that if a White celebrity were to come out and say they wanted to adopt a child but only wanted a White child, many people would call that racist. I don't understand why it's anyone's business or why anyone would care about Charlize Theron adopting a child, but if it does matter, shouldn't we be happy that a child is getting a good home — regardless of race? Some say that a White person cannot raise a Black child. Others have said that the child would eventually revert to its innate Black characteristics. So, a Black baby is destined to be poorly educated, lazy, violent, and speak slang even if raised by Whites. Even the glory of the parent's 'Whiteness' won't be enough to overcome these inherent differences. Obviously this is absurd, but when accepted as the truth, that is what is being said. If

70

someone believes this, even in lieu of feeling superior over another race, he or she is exhibiting racism.

Here's one that really confused me. A friend told me she doesn't watch the Grammys because it's not Black enough. On the day following the award show, a talk show host on a Black radio station said that she believed there was a systematic 'Whitening' of the Grammys. She said that in the tribute to Etta James, she was offended that they had Bonnie Raitt singing because she's not a soul singer.[31] One caller said he liked the show, especially the performance by Bruno Mars. The radio host said Bruno was okay, but he's not Black. She also mentioned being bothered by the fact that Martina McBride and Florence Welch were on stage to honor Aretha Franklin the year before, but she was somehow okay with Christina Aguilera.[32]

She felt that with the exception of Adele, most of the White artist couldn't really sing and that the industry as a whole wanted to find as many Whites with a little talent and teach them to sing with a little bit of soul so they could replace the Black artists. This is the paranoia of which I speak. No one said anything about race or did anything racist, but she saw race in the Grammys.

This 'race is in everything' paranoia and selfishness is far more common than many would believe. I've had many Black people over the years say things about Whites, such as, "That's what they think about us," or, "You know what they say." This is a perfect example of what I mean. They would look at me as if I was crazy when I asked, "Do you really think Whites sit around thinking about Blacks?" For some, the answer is, "Yes."

This is like those who say that Blues and Jazz music is Black music and that the Whites stole it, yet when you go to Blues and

Jazz clubs throughout America, there are lots of White and Black artists playing, but there are no Blacks in the audience.[33] This reminds me of a conversation I had with Blues legend Buddy Guy.

I went to Buddy Guy's Legends, a popular Blues club in Chicago owned by legendary Blues artist Buddy Guy. We had met a couple of times before, and on that day he was celebrating the recent release of a new career-spanning boxed set which coincided with his 70th birthday a few months earlier. After securing a signed copy of the boxed set, we sat at the bar, talking before the crowd came in. We started to talk about music, and as he began to wax nostalgic about his career, he wondered what was in store for the future of Blues. He then told me an interesting story.

He told me he'd had a gig at a casino one weekend and was walking through the casino floor prior to the show when a young White girl ran up to him. She was with a friend, a young Black girl around the same age. The White girl was excited to see him and asked if she could take a picture with him. Her Black friend, who was obviously confused by this exchange, asked who the man was, and when the White girl told her, Buddy could tell that the Black girl had never heard of him. He said to the Black girl, "You're probably familiar with my daughter Shawnna," and sure enough, when he said her name, the Black girl knew her immediately and said she loved her.

He went on about how he's seen a dramatic change over his career, how so few Blacks come to the shows, and how those who do come are older. "Young Blacks don't know the Blues", Buddy said. I agreed and said that he would be surprised that I had never heard of his daughter, and, almost on cue, she walked into the club. He introduced us and she was very nice. A small group of us sat and chatted for about an hour or so before the show started. The remainder of our conversation was mostly small talk, and his daughter Shawnna was refreshingly polite and somewhat demure. After the show, I called my best friend who was an authority on all things Hip-Hop and R&B and asked him if he had ever heard of Shawnna. Let me just say that I was extremely surprised when he told me who she is and the type of music she sings.[34]

This is another example of our selfishness. We want to claim music as our own even when we don't support it. Blues, Jazz, and Rock 'n' Roll are all types of music that we say Whites stole from us, but we seldom listen to this music, even when Blacks are performing it.

While listening to WVON, Matt McGill had a topic on his show that asked, "Who's the bigger sellout: a Black man married to a White woman or a Black Republican?" After polling the callers, it wasn't even close — it was the Black Republican hands down. This label of sellout has been thrown around for years and prevents Conservative-minded Blacks from openly stating their views. This assertion doesn't make sense. Even understanding the brazen selfishness of people, it is still shocking that most Blacks believe that if you are Black then you have to share their beliefs, and if you don't, then you are turning your back on the entire race.

While claiming music as 'Black', calling other Blacks sellouts, and calling mixed-race people Black are examples of Blacks being selfish; it's also bad for the fight against racism. Group-think is a powerful thing, and if other Blacks feel pressured to conform to this concept, then it has a limiting effect on the actions some should take as well as the amount of overall knowledge and understanding they might gain about the issues. When the Tea

Party and some Republicans say, "We want to take back the country," Blacks automatically make that about race. I've heard people say that they believe it means the extremists want to take the country back to the days of the Jim Crow South. It's clear that the belief that most Whites are racist negatively affects how we view things. We have to get past these views.

It is imperative for the country that we begin to make real strides in improving race relations. This cannot happen if Blacks continue to suspect all Whites and if Whites remain afraid to talk openly about race, or, worse yet, if Whites completely ignore Blacks. We must wake up and realize that these feelings of prejudice are not innate, but that they are learned. In many cases, they don't even exist — they are just assumed.

As the great Black abolitionist Frederick Douglass once said, "Some people will have it that there is a natural, an inherent, and an invincible repugnance in the breast of the White race toward dark-colored people; and some very intelligent colored men think that their proscription is owing solely to the color which nature has given them. They hold that they are rated according to their color, and that it is impossible for White people ever to look upon dark races of men, or men belonging to the African race, with other than feelings of aversion. My experience, both serious and mirthful, combats this conclusion."[35]

If a man who grew up as a slave in the segregated South of the 1800s could realize that all Whites aren't racist, then why can't free Blacks in the 21st century realize it? Racism still exists, and we need to address it directly. We cannot move forward as a race by harboring resentment toward Whites or by suspecting that race is the primary issue in every incident.

74

Which Party is Racist?

Because of the history of Blacks in America, it is understandable that civil rights have played an enormously important role in how we vote. How Blacks are treated during a presidency, and the role that the administration assumes on race relations, have traditionally had an impact on how we vote as a group greater than any other issues. We are told that Abraham Lincoln was a Republican and that he freed the slaves, but we are also told that there was a shift within the Republican Party during the Civil Rights Movement of the 1950s and 1960s when many of the White racist Democrats of the South joined the Republican Party. What I found is that it is not logical to assume that all racist Democrats switched parties or that the Republicans did not support the Civil Rights Movement.

Looking at the history of both parties from a logical point of view has caused me to wonder why Blacks vote almost unanimously for the Democratic Party. Here are some facts about how each president from Abraham Lincoln to Lyndon Baines Johnson approached racial issues and how the parties were affected by their actions.

The Republican Party was founded by anti-slavery activists, and in 1856 John Fremont won the party's first presidential nomination running on a platform that included a crusade against the expansion of slavery.[36] Four years later, Abraham Lincoln would win the presidential election, becoming the first Republican to hold the office. The Southern states succeeded from the Union shortly after his inauguration, leading to the Civil War. He would later pass the 13th Amendment[37] and forever be known as the man who freed the slaves.

The end of the Civil War saw a lengthy hold on the presidency by Republicans. Between Lincoln and FDR, there were fourteen presidents, only three of whom were Democrats: Andrew Johnson, Grover Cleveland, and Woodrow Wilson. Andrew Johnson was chosen by the delegates as Lincoln's Vice Presidential running mate for his second term to add balance to the ticket. This gave Lincoln a large majority over his opponent.[38] Johnson became president when Lincoln was assassinated, meaning he was never elected to the office. He twice vetoed the Civil Rights Act of 1866[39] and became the first president to be impeached. The second was William J. Clinton, also a Democrat.

Cleveland was reluctant to enforce the 15th Amendment[40] and chided Chinese immigrants for being unwilling to assimilate into White society.[41] He would later lobby Congress to pass the Scott Act that would prevent Chinese immigrants who left the United States from returning.[42]

Woodrow Wilson expanded segregationist policies,[43] did nothing to stop segregation within his departments,[44] and while president of Princeton, he discouraged Blacks from applying.[45]

As for the eleven Republican presidents during this period, most had a platform that focused on civil rights, and all were endorsed by the majority of the Black population, although McKinley did not do much and lost much of his Black support. Grant prosecuted Klan members,[46] became the first president to sign a civil rights act,[47] and passed the 15th Amendment allowing Blacks the right to vote.[48] Garfield was the first to try to use federal funds to focus specifically on the education of Blacks,[49] and Teddy Roosevelt created a controversy by inviting Booker T. Washington to the White House for dinner.[50] Though Harding's presidency was rife with scandal, he advocated for full civil rights for Blacks and women during his presidential campaign, and once elected, he delivered a speech condemning lynching and supporting the Dyer Anti-lynching Bill in 1921,[51] Coolidge became president at a time when the Klan had great numbers. He fought for Blacks and denounced the Klan, causing them to lose much of their power. He also appointed Blacks to judgeships and other prominent posts.[52]

There were two historic moments that contributed to the shift in alliance with the Republican Party concerning the Black vote. The first came during Franklin Delano Roosevelt's Administration. The other occurred over thirty years later.

The New Deal was enacted as an effort to provide immediate relief from the Great Depression. It is generally referred to in two parts; the New Deal and the Second New Deal.[53] Initially, the New Deal focused primarily on the financial sector and businesses. The Second New Deal increased the scope of the initial regulations. Under this plan, the Social Security Act, National Labor Relations Act, and the Fair Labor Standards Act of 1938 were implemented. In addition, the Works Progress Administration and the United States

Housing Authority were also created.[54] While the New Deal of 1933 had majority support, the Second New Deal had many detractors.

Many Republicans and Conservative Democrats thought it was an overreach of government, equating it to Socialism. Because Blacks eventually saw some benefit both from the relief programs as well as from the jobs programs, they made a dramatic shift of support to Roosevelt. Many also started to think that since Republicans opposed the New Deal, which was helping them, Republicans no longer supported the progress of Blacks. The Republican Party would never gain the majority of the Black vote again.

Because FDR implemented these far-reaching programs doesn't mean that he was all about racial equality. Although there is no doubt that the New Deal was helpful to Blacks in the short term,[55] it was implemented to battle the results of the Great Depression, and there is no evidence that Roosevelt listed assistance to Blacks as a goal of the New Deal. He also did little to assuage racial discrimination, and he refused to pass anti-lynching legislation. He later issued Executive Order 9066 which relocated Japanese Americans to internment camps. Although this did not directly affect Blacks, over 100,000 people, mostly American citizens, were also interned.[56] This was hardly inclusive.

Upon FDR's death, Truman ascended to the presidency. He issued Executive Order 9981 in 1948, which desegregated the Armed Forces.[57] He also issued executive orders making discrimination in civil service positions and defense contracts illegal.[58]

Dwight Eisenhower was president at the onset of the Civil Rights Movement. Eisenhower, a Republican and former five-star general, signed the Civil Rights Act of 1957 and 1960 into law, establishing a permanent civil rights office inside the Justice Department.[59] The 1957 bill was challenged by many Democrats, including Strom Thurmond. The South Carolina Senator conducted a filibuster against the bill, speaking for 24 hours and 18 minutes, the longest filibuster to date.[60] Eisenhower also sent the National Guard to Arkansas when the governor refused to obey the ruling of Brown v. Board of Education,[61] and he expanded upon many of the provisions of the New Deal.

Although Truman had desegregated the armed forces by executive order, it had not been implemented. Eisenhower actually enforced the order and vowed to make true and rapid progress in civil rights and equality of employment opportunity in his 1953 State of the Union Address.[62]

Kennedy's presidency had mixed results on the race issue. He believed that civil rights issues were important but thought the methods of Martin Luther King, Jr. and others would make it difficult to pass laws advocating civil rights, so he was initially slow to act. As president, he did, however, facilitate King's release from jail in Georgia, which garnered support from Blacks during his presidency. He ordered protection for the Freedom Riders, who rode buses to challenge segregation, but he urged them to stop their protests.

Kennedy used force at the University of Mississippi in 1962 and the University of Alabama in 1963 when Black students were prevented from entering. After the University of Alabama incident, he gave a national address on civil rights.[63] Although he declined an invitation to speak at the March on Washington, he supported the March and gave hundreds of thousands of dollars to the sponsors.[64] Later, in 1963, based on allegations from J. Edgar Hoover, he authorized the FBI to wiretap King's conversations.[65]

The second and most dramatic shift of the Black vote happened in 1964. After Kennedy's assassination in November 1963, Lyndon Johnson ascended to the presidency. In July of the following year, Johnson passed the most sweeping advances in civil rights since the Civil War. Using his southern influence to sway some Democrats, he passed the Civil Rights Act of 1964.[66] While he is credited for the success of this bill, it is important to note that there was much resistance from Democrats, including a famous filibuster by Robert Byrd,[67] while most of the support came from Republicans. The bill received over 80% approval from Republicans in the House and Senate compared to just over 61% approval from Democrats.[68] Johnson would later also pass the Voting Rights Act of 1965.[69]

At the same time Johnson was fighting for civil rights, there was a tight battle brewing as to who would become his opponent for the presidency that fall. The fight was between New York Governor Nelson Rockefeller and Arizona Senator Barry Goldwater. Although the race was close and Rockefeller had more support, a Rockefeller scandal gave Goldwater the nomination.[70] This created a stark contrast between the two candidates.

Republican Barry Goldwater had written in 1960, *The Conscience of a Conservative*, a book meant to be a template for the Republican platform. A staunch Conservative, he disagreed with most Progressive Conservatives and advocated states' rights, strict adherence to the Constitution, and limited federal government regulations. His views were seen as being against everything the Civil Rights Movement was trying to accomplish.

80

In the 1964 election, voters had the choice of Johnson, the incumbent who openly advocated social programs, and Goldwater, the strict Constitutionalist who refused to soften his Conservative views. Johnson won in a landslide, but what's more important from the perspective of racial views is that he received an unprecedented 94% of the Black vote.

This changed how Blacks voted going forward. Although there had been a shift away from their allegiance to the Republican Party during FDR's 'reign', Republicans had still received a sizable portion of the Black vote. Eisenhower got 39% of the Black vote, and Nixon got 32% in his 1960 loss to Kennedy.[71] Since Goldwater's loss in 1964, no other Republican has received more than 15% of the Black vote. Nevertheless, does Goldwater's Conservative stance prove that Republicans had become what the Democrats of the 19th century had been?

This would be a drastic shift in ideology, and it would not be logical to believe that Republicans just changed their views overnight. Many believe that although the Democrats displayed more racism than Republicans, particularly in the South, most of these racist Democrats moved to the Republican Party in the 1950s and 1960s. There is really no solid evidence of this. In 1964 and 1965, more Republicans voted for the civil rights and voting rights bills than Democrats. If there was a shift, it seemed to be based more on the size of government than on race relations. You cannot prove a negative, and while the Republicans can't definitively say that none of the racist Democrats were openly embraced by them, the Democrats can't prove that all of the racists left their party nor can it be assumed that the Republicans who fought for civil rights joined the Democratic Party. It is also important to note that when

Blacks shifted their alliance to the Democratic Party, it was not due to racism on the part of Republicans. Blacks moved away from the Republican Party because of the programs the Democrats were implementing and not because of the Republican's racist beliefs. It has been said that there's no such thing as a free lunch. Blacks received assistance from programs they thought were designed to help them, but, regardless of the intent of the programs, they are still paying for those programs today.

Part III
POLITICS

Political Beginnings

My introduction into politics was probably the same as it was for most Blacks. I turned 18, was told that I had to vote since my ancestors had fought for me to have that right, and was told to vote Democrat. I never bothered to question why. In fact, I really didn't know what being a Democrat or a Republican meant. I just knew that Democrats were the good guys.

I was too young to vote in the 1988 presidential election, but it was the first time I watched a presidential race. It was interesting to see the candidates debate a wide array of issues and try to differentiate themselves from the others in the primaries. This was a perfect year to get inaugurated into national politics because it was the end of Reagan's second term, and since he couldn't run again, there were primaries on both sides. There had to be at least 20 people running that year.[72][73]

Once the primaries were over and each party had made its nomination, the tone of the election seemed to change. The candidates seemed to spend more time attacking each other than they did trying to show that they were the better candidate. The Bush campaign ran the infamous Willie Horton ad, while Dukakis' deputy field director demanded that Bush fess up to an extramarital affair that she alleged he'd had with his assistant. All of this was acted out on TV. This would turn out to be the new norm in political campaigns.

In 1990 I voted for the first time. It was nothing like the glitz and glamour of the presidential election I had seen in 1988. It was a midterm election, so I didn't get to see all of the commercials, campaigning, and debates. First the primaries came, and a long list of candidates I didn't know were on the ballot. I heard my mom and other people talking about some of them, so I voted for those names that were now familiar, but when the general election came, it was much easier; I just pulled the lever to pick all of the Democrats and walked out.

By 1992, I was ready to finally cast my first vote for a presidential candidate, and there was no doubt for whom I was voting. I was Black so I favored the Democrats. The economy was bad, and President Bush had gone back on his promise not to raise taxes. I didn't know whether this was a good or bad thing, but it didn't matter — he'd gone back on his word — so he couldn't be trusted. After Clinton won, I went back to my everyday life and didn't think much about politics.

I was back in my hometown of Gary from school and started to notice a change in the community. Crime was up, while businesses were closing, and the city was starting to look run down. Back in the mid-eighties, U.S. Steel, the largest employer in town, had a major layoff. The city never recovered, but it seemed even worse in the nineties so I started to wonder what the local government was doing.

Speaking of local government, it is obvious that most of the legislation that directly affects us happens on the state and local levels. While national politics gets all of the glamour, the real work is done closer to home. Much of the federal legislation serves as guidelines, leaving the states to implement it.[74] Whether the issue is welfare reform, education, or TARP, and regardless of how much money the federal government votes to dole out, the funds are managed and dispersed by state and local officials.[75] So I find it odd that many people pay attention to national politics and totally ignore local and statewide concerns. In fact, there are a number of people who only vote in presidential elections. Whether they blame Bush or praise Obama for the outcome of federal programs, they don't give any credence to the actions of their local politicians. This shows that a large percentage of the population doesn't understand how the government works, and it is just one more example of how people are not using logic when they vote.

In 1995, Attorney Scott King, a White man, became Mayor of Gary, Indiana, besting three Black candidates.[76] It became such a big story that it garnered national news coverage. You see, Gary had the highest percentage of Blacks of any city in the country. In 1967, they had elected one of the first three Black men to become mayor of a major city, as Cleveland and Washington DC had also elected Black mayors that year.[77] Every mayor in Gary from that election up to 1995 had been Black. This was one of the few times that Blacks broke away from the "Vote for the Black candidate" mantra, but if you look closely, there was still an ugly stereotype at play.

When asked why they voted for Scott King, the White candidate, many Blacks were quoted as saying, "As a White man, he will be better equipped to deal with the politicians in the capital." So, were they saying that he would be better equipped because the Black candidates weren't as capable as the White candidate? Or, were

87

they saying that the politicians in Indianapolis, mostly Republicans, were racist and would be more apt to listen to a White man. I assume the latter, but in any case, there was no basis for their argument. This is because there is no proof that the politicians were racist, nor was there proof that if they were, they would listen to Scott King solely because he was White. I am not questioning his effectiveness as mayor. Regardless of why Blacks voted for him, he may have been the best person for the job. The problem isn't that he won; the problem is that many people let their assumptions dictate how they voted rather than the candidates' qualifications.

When it came time for my next presidential election, I was discouraged by what I had seen locally from the Democratic Party, but I still had no reason to see the Republicans as a viable option. Although I was starting to pay more attention to how my politicians performed, I still had no point of reference for the Republicans. 1996 marked the fourth election in which I would participate, and I had yet to see a Republican candidate on the ballot, with the exception of presidential and gubernatorial candidates, and none of them came to my area to campaign. As far as the presidential election was concerned, I thought the economy was doing well and didn't see a reason to make a change. I voted for Bill Clinton once more in 1996, and he won again.

Over the next few years, things changed for me. I started to pay attention to the news between the presidential election cycles and focus more on the role of government in our lives. Living in a predominantly Black neighborhood, all of our local politicians were Democrats. I started to notice that I didn't agree with many of their policies. I felt they wanted to regulate too much of our lives. I searched for alternatives, but none seemed to be available. When

I did hear the policies suggested by the Republicans, they didn't seem to be extreme; however, when it came time for an election, the Republicans were trounced. That is, if they had a candidate at all. When I asked why no one ever considered voting for a Republican candidate, I was told, "You can't vote for them; they're racist." This did not seem valid to me, so I started to do some research to determine where this assumption came from.

In many of our races, the Republicans didn't even field a candidate. When I looked at both parties issue by issue, I found that I didn't feel I agreed with either party enough to say I was a Democrat or a Republican. I was now an Independent but I continued to register as a Democrat. Since the Republicans rarely had a candidate, the Democrat who won the primary was all but guaranteed a victory in the general election. I registered as a Democrat so that I would be able to help choose the candidate who would eventually win.

After years of being told that our Black vote for Democrats was in our best interests, I began to realize that we didn't all have the same best interests. I also didn't see how their policies were helping. While I was moving away from Democrats locally, overall, I had no affinity for either party due to the lack of participation of Republicans in my area. So when the 2000 presidential candidates were announced, it was not nearly as easy for me to decide as it had been in the past.

The Democrats, who were proponents of the government controls I was questioning, gave us Al Gore. He was the husband of the woman from the Parents Music Resource Center who wanted to censor music and control individual consumption. The Republicans gave us George W. Bush. He was the son of the president I had helped to vote out of office during my first presidential election. Why would I want to vote for the child of a previous president? Were we moving toward a dynasty? I also started to see the advocates from both parties as angry and distrustful.

The 2000 election turned out to be the closest presidential election since 1876 and the most hotly contested.[78] It created hatred toward the president as we had never seen and virtually split the country in two. It also created a massive image problem for the Republicans that they are still trying to overcome twelve years later. In spite of all of this, I could not have been more disengaged by these two candidates. In fact, this was the only time I voted for a third-party candidate in a presidential election, Harry Browne, the Libertarian Party candidate.[79]

As my personal beliefs were being honed, I searched for a better understanding of what the parties stood for. You would think the best place to go for this information was the parties themselves. What I actually got was misdirection and confusion. It seemed to me that both parties spent more time denigrating the opposing party then they did pushing their own agendas. What I found was confusing rhetoric within both parties being used to gain support to the detriment of its opponents. There was also a power struggle between the parties, and often within the parties, which sometimes became more important than what was best for the country. It has been ingrained in each member of both parties to attack the other party. In the eyes of either party, "When the other party is in control, we're losing."

When Senate Minority Leader Mitch McConnell told Major Garrett of the *National Journal*, "The single most important thing we want to achieve is for President Obama to be a one-term president," it was a foolish thing to say, but it was true. It was foolish because it was perceived as selfish and unpatriotic. It made it look as if the Republicans were putting the party before the country, and to many, it looked racist. But in reality, it is always the most important thing the party on the outside wants to achieve. If this wasn't the case, why would the opposing party nominate a candidate to run against a sitting president who is extremely popular?

Think about it. It costs millions of dollars to run a presidential campaign, and no president has ever lost re-election when his approval rating was better than 45%. Look at the historic approval ratings of all presidents seeking re-elections as far back as data is available:[80]

Presidential Approval
Leading to Presidential Elections
(Based on monthly averages of approval ratings)

	8 months before election	6 months before election	2 months before election
	%	%	%
1940 (Roosevelt)	57	60	NA
1948 (Truman)	36	–	NA
1956 (Eisenhower)	69	73	NA
1964 (Johnson)	75	74	NA
1972 (Nixon)	54	58	NA
1976 (Ford)	48	45	NA
1980 (Carter)	39	32	37
1984 (Reagan)	54	54	56
1992 (Bush 41)	41	37	38
1996 (Clinton)	55	55	60

So, based on this info, why run a candidate against Roosevelt, Eisenhower, Johnson, Nixon, Reagan, or Clinton? Power and control can be the only reason that the opposing parties didn't say, "The country is clearly happy with the president. Let's just save the money and time we would spend on a campaign and reach across the aisle and work with him." Take a look at the incumbents listed above. There were three Republicans and three Democrats. It doesn't matter which party is in power; the other party wants that power. Often a president will have a decision attacked by the opposing party. Many times the opposition has an honest difference in ideology, while other times it's simply a power play. Making the other party look bad is believed to be helpful for one's own party. While the actions of our politicians are supposed to be for 'The People', we find that they often have an ulterior motive.

Speaking of 'The People', the number of people who don't vote is surprisingly interesting. I have always known that there was a segment of the population who did not vote, but I had no idea it was so large. When Barak Obama won the Democratic nomination in 2008, his was a transformational candidacy that drove many to the polls who had never voted before. Imagine my surprise when I found out that the voter turnout for that election was only around 63%. You would think that it would be in the higher 70th or lower 80th percentile. This piqued my interest, so I researched historical voter turnout stats and was shocked by the results. From 1840 to 1908, voter turnout for presidential elections averaged 75.6% with a high in 1876 of nearly 82%. Since 1912, it has never been higher than 63%, and the 63% in 2008 was the first time voter turnout had been greater than 60% in forty years. Some attribute the drop after 1968 to the lowering of the voting age from 21 to 18. This may have had some effect, however, prior to 1968, the average turnout had already dropped to 58.3%.[81]The fact that the rally of 2008 only increased turnout to 63% is a bit alarming. Compare this to the average voter turnout in 20 other countries:[82]

Turnout in national lower house elections
1960–1995

Austria	92%
Iceland	89%
New Zealand	88%
Denmark	87%
Germany	86%
Sweden	86%
Czech Republic	85%
Costa Rica	81%
Norway	81%
Romania	81%
Bulgaria	80%
Israel	80%
Portugal	79%
Finland	78%
France	76%
United Kingdom	76%
South Korea	75%
Ireland	74%
Canada	74%
Spain	73%
United States	**48%**

This list excludes any countries with compulsory voting during that period. As you can see, U.S. voter turnout is far less than most other countries. Even if we only count presidential elections, the U.S. turnout would only go up to 55%. This would still leave almost half of the eligible voters out of the process. Why would so many people choose not to vote?

There are many factors that may contribute to the lack of voter turnout. Some people never take the time to register to vote, while others change their minds at the last minute due to weather, traffic, or long lines at the polls. Many choose not to vote because they believe that their vote doesn't count or that there is no difference between the candidates, causing them to grow apathetic about the election. Although these and several other factors may affect the voter turnout, the lies and confusing rhetoric created by both parties is the primary reason for the lack of interest. In their effort to get voters to change their minds, politicians tend to lose sight of what they want to do and only focus on attacking their opponent. Among the many methods politicians choose to attack their opponents and sway voters, the two most often used are either an ad hominem attack or they use a lie of omission. This type of politics isn't new. In fact, I'm sure politicians have been twisting words and attacking their opponents for as long as there have been elections. The major change is in the way we receive our news. Because of the Internet and the 24-hour news cycle, there is an endless stream of information. Since most of us are too busy to read and research it all, we now get our news updates from sound bites. This has created a culture of 'The best sound bite wins' for most politicians. If you have a great message but can't condense it, most people will never get that message. This also upped the ante on the attacks. Now, we hear them all repeated in rapid succession. With most of us not verifying the information, it becomes fact and may cause many to change their votes. Like it or not, if it wasn't effective, then the politicians would not use them.

The ad hominem attack is obvious by its glaring nature; however, it gets continued use because people pay attention to it. To work, it only needs two components. It needs to be bombastic enough to get media attention, and there needs to be a segment of the population that is vehemently turned off by the alleged behavior or stance on any issue. With these two ingredients, the attack can, at the very least, turn around a few votes. At extremes, it can cause movements or rallies. Politically these attacks occur on both sides, but they are only noticed by the voters when they are leveled toward their candidate. If you call President Obama a Socialist, then the Democrats are up in arms but the Republicans don't have a problem with that; that is, until Kanye West says, "George Bush doesn't care about Black people."[83]

Everything takes us back to logic. We hear a story and, based on our personal feelings, we get upset or we are in total agreement. The problem we run into is, if we don't listen impartially and make logical assertions, then we run the risk of missing the truth. Although the personal attacks are bad, they are minimal when compared to the lies of omission. This is what I find we are being served by politicians and the media on a regular basis. As are the personal attacks, these lies of omission are also committed by both parties, but here they have help from the media. Many will tell you that the media likes to pick sides based on their political affiliations, which is definitely the case. However, the one thing they seem to care more about is ratings, and if they can create a story that will give them a ratings boost, then they would do almost anything — including editing stories in a way that makes them more sensational.

Earlier, I mentioned that Mitch McConnell's comment about making Obama a one-term president was foolish — but was it really? It was a bad political move because he should have known how the media would use his statement. But did he really say what we think he said? This gives us a great example of how the lies of omission work. We've all heard the story; it was run constantly on the news that McConnell said that making Obama a one-term president was the most important for him to do, implying that it was more important than passing laws, fixing the economy, and in any way moving the country forward. Here's the problem; it's not entirely true. Things sound different when taken out of context. Here's a greater portion of the interview:

NJ – You've been studying the history of presidents who lost part or all of Congress in their first term. Why?

McConnell – In the last 100 years, three presidents suffered big defeats in Congress in their first term and then won reelection: Harry Truman, Dwight Eisenhower, and the most recent example, Bill Clinton. I read a lot of history anyway, but I am trying to apply those lessons to current situations in hopes of not making the same mistakes.

NJ – What have you learned?

McConnell – After 1994, the public had the impression we Republicans over promised and under delivered. We suffered from some degree of hubris and acted as if the president was irrelevant and we would roll over him. By the summer of 1995, he was already on the way to being reelected, and we were hanging on for our lives.

NJ – What does this mean now?

McConnell – We need to be honest with the public. This election is about them, not us. And we need to treat this election as the first step in retaking the government. We need to say to everyone on Election Day, "Those of you who helped make this a good day, you need to go out and help us finish the job."

NJ – What's the job?

McConnell – The single most important thing we want to achieve is for President Obama to be a one-term president.

NJ – Does that mean endless, or at least frequent, confrontation with the president?

McConnell – If President Obama does a Clintonian back flip, if he's willing to meet us halfway on some of the biggest issues, it's not inappropriate for us to do business with him.

NJ – What are the big issues?

McConnell – It is possible the president's advisers will tell him he has to do something to get right with the public on his levels of spending and [on] lowering the national debt. If he were to heed that advice, he would, I imagine, find more support among our conference than he would among some in the Senate in his own party. I don't want the president to fail; I want him to change. So, we'll see. The next move is going to be up to him.

NJ – What will you seek from the president on the tax issue?

McConnell – At the very least, I believe we should extend all of the Bush tax cuts. And I prefer to describe this as keeping current tax policy. It's been on the books for 10 years. Now, how long that [extension] is, is something we can discuss. It was clear his position was not [favored] among all Senate Democrats. They had their own divisions. I don't think those divisions are going to be any less in November and December.[84]

All of the news outlets left out the fact that he and the interviewer were talking about the midterm elections where the Republicans won back the House. And, yes, he did say to the people who helped them gain seats that their job wasn't done and that they needed help to make sure Obama lost the next election; however, is it fair to leave out the part where he specifically said that in 1994 the Republicans acted as if the president was irrelevant and that they *could not* repeat that mistake? This was vastly different from what the media portrayed him as having said.

The media are amateurs compared to the politicians. It is quite natural for them to take the facts that support their views and those that make their opponent look bad and make carefully crafted statements they can use to beat us over the head, knowing that these statements will be repeated on all the news outlets. Unfortunately, they care more about being able to match the information with their views than they do about how factual the information is. If they can infer what they want from a portion of the information available but the sum of the information weakens their point, then why not just omit the portion that doesn't fit? Here are just a few examples of how politicians manipulate facts they present to us.

At the Republican National Convention, Paul Ryan said that while campaigning in 2008, Obama said that a GM plant in Janesville, Wisconsin would be around for another 100 years with government support.[85] The plant failed, and many attacked Paul Ryan for the comments at the convention, saying that he was implying it was Obama's fault the plant closed, and Ryan's critics cited the fact that the plant had closed before Obama even became president. This is true and the reason why half-truths are also considered lies. Ryan was right, but his comment would have been more effective if he didn't leave room for opponents to guess what he was implying. While the plant did close prior to his taking office, Obama said that the government should help GM, and that with government support, the plant would be around for another 100 years. GM got the bailout Obama supported, but they still closed that plant.[86] The fact that the bailout was implemented by Bush doesn't change this. Ryan should have pointed out that President Obama was wrong in his belief that if the government assisted GM, then the plant would remain open. Again, whether the bailout worked or not can be debated. What's important is noting how the so-called fact checkers were able to label Ryan's statement as a lie.

Conversely, at the Democratic National Convention, Bill Clinton said that Paul Ryan's proposed budget would raise taxes on the middle class by $2,000. The Obama campaign even ran an ad stating the same facts. The problem is that we have no way of knowing. The assumption was that in order for Romney to implement his tax cuts and not create more debt, he would have to cut several exemptions and deductions the middle class usually take, thus costing them an average of $2,000 per year. This may or may not be true; however, Clinton has no way of knowing which exemptions and deductions, if any, Romney would cut. Therefore, he can't know if it will raise taxes, how much taxes would be raised, or whose taxes would be raised. Yet, Bill Clinton stated the figure of $2,000 as if it were a fact.[87]

Then, there is the debate over social security. Each side drastically decried the other and used emotion in an effort to affect how people would vote. The Obama campaign accused Romney of wanting to throw seniors off a cliff or, at the very least, turning social security over to Wall Street. Although both Romney and Ryan had supported allowing a percentage of social security benefits to be held in private accounts, it was unfair to equate this with turning social security over to Wall Street. The private accounts would have allowed recipients to invest retirement funds which could have led to additional gains or losses, but there's no evidence that this would have been mandatory. It would have simply offered additional flexibility, including the ability to pass the money along to their beneficiaries.[88]

On the other side, the Romney campaign accused Obama of cutting benefits by as much as 25%. This was also a distortion of the truth. If all things remain the same, the social security trust fund would be solvent for about 20 years, meaning that no one currently on social security would lose benefits; also, based on the current administration's penchant to raise taxes, there's all but a guarantee that Obama would raise taxes to fund social security.[89]

Something needs to be done to fix social security for everyone else, and it's clear that neither party has a solution, but one thing is certain: Distorting the facts about our problems is bad for both parties and bad for America.

The most highly-debated topic this election cycle had to be taxing the rich. The debate for and against each side's views were hard-fought, mean-spirited, and divisive. They used varying reports and facts to skew information about tax codes, income levels, etc. They even had varying statistics on how much of the country supports their views. Then, on July 13, 2012, the fight was kicked up several notches. While campaigning in Virginia, Obama said this:[90]

> "There are a lot of wealthy, successful Americans who agree with me — because they want to give something back. They know they didn't — look, if you've been successful, you didn't get there on your own. You didn't get there on your own. I'm always struck by people who think, well, it must be because I was just so smart. There are a lot of smart people out there. It must be because I worked harder than everybody else. Let me tell you something — there are a whole bunch of hardworking people out there.
>
> If you were successful, somebody along the line gave you some help. There was a great teacher somewhere in your life. Somebody helped to create this unbelievable American system that we have [sic] that allowed you to thrive. Somebody invested in roads and bridges. If you've got a business —

you didn't build that. Somebody else made that happen. The Internet didn't get invented on its own. Government research created the Internet so that all the companies could make money off the Internet.

The point is, is that when we succeed, we succeed because of our individual initiative, but also because we do things together. There are some things, just like fighting fires, we don't do on our own. I mean, imagine if everybody had their own fire service. That would be a hard way to organize fighting fires."

After this campaign speech, the spin machine started. Almost immediately, Republican politicians and pundits began accusing Obama of being anti-business. There were commercials, websites, and blogs dedicated to the comment, "You didn't build that." It became a staple on the campaign trail for Romney/Ryan, and it was mentioned repeatedly at the Republican National Convention. As for the Obama campaign, they said the phrase was simply taken out of context and that he was speaking of roads and bridges. After reading the comments in their context, I have to side with the Obama campaign. That particular phrase was meant to imply that business owners didn't build their businesses alone and didn't build the roads. Telling business owners that Obama said, "You didn't build that," sounds good in a sound bite but is disingenuous and is no better than the Democrats who twisted Mitt Romney's words in a January 9, 2012 speech.[91]

At a breakfast in New Hampshire, while talking about healthcare, Romney said, "I like being able to fire people who provide services to me; you know, if someone doesn't give me the good service that I need, I want to say, I'm going to go get someone else to provide that service to me." The sound bite that later ran constantly on news programs was, "I like being able to fire people . . ." This misrepresented what he'd actually said.[92]

Saying that Obama is anti-business backfired against the Republicans in two ways. First, there's a considerable percentage of the population that was anti-business, so they don't see this as a smear. Secondly, it helped Democrats to further sell the stereotype that Republicans fight primarily for big business. Never mind the fact that Obama received more donations from big business than Romney did. However, the biggest problem with the Republican attacks on the "You didn't build that" comment was that it didn't address the real point on which they should have been focused — Obama was wrong. To fairly analyze the statement, it needs to be looked at in two separate sections in order to decipher what the intent was:

1 – Needing help to be successful
2 – The government's role in our basic needs

First, while it is unfair to say that Obama was talking about businesses when he said, "You didn't build that," it is also illogical to use conjecture to determine his intent or the campaign's attempt to imply that his comment was solely about roads and bridges. Just before the much talked about line, Obama said, "If you were successful, somebody along the line gave you some help." He is correct here, and no one can dispute this statement. He mentioned a great teacher, but it goes far beyond that. Take any innovator or business owner; in addition to any help they received in education, they borrowed money from a family member, had help with other parts of the business they didn't know, got inspiration from another entrepreneur's prior invention, etc. Perhaps they even had a spouse sacrifice and support the family so that they could achieve their dream. However it happened, Obama is right that there was help along the line.

As for the second part, Obama said, "Somebody invested in roads and bridges." He went on to point to the Internet and fighting fires as things the government has done. He was implying that now that you are successful, you need to pay for that. Again, his points are based on facts. The government did build the roads and bridges. They also fight fires, provide us with security, and the government is deemed responsible for many other useful things. Here is what is interesting about the statement when taken in its entirety. Split the comment into two parts and you will see that each part alone is true. This may lead you to ask, "How can he be wrong?" Earlier, I said that the Republicans should have focused on the fact that Obama was wrong, and then I went on to demonstrate how his statements were true. This is why Obama is successful as a speaker and why I thought the Republicans were right to attack the comments but were going about it in the wrong way.

The statement taken as a whole presents a basic non sequitur. Though the two statements alone are logical, when combined they create a false conclusion. While there may be many wealthy Americans who agree that they should give back and that the government plays a basic role in important needs, the fact that the wealthy should pay more in taxes is not the logical conclusion. We all have a duty to give back, money or time, to those in need, but the government should not be able to force people to do it. If it's true that these successful people owe a debt to those who helped them, wouldn't they owe it to their friends, family, business partners, or whomever helped them along the way? The great teacher was paid for those services and is owed nothing more. Unless the president is suggesting that we pay a vig to our teachers when we grow up, based on how successful we have become, this doesn't make sense.

Next, Obama implied that the government plays an active role in the success of wealthy Americans and therefore they should be taxed for that. Can it really be argued that business owners use more of the roads than the rest of the population? This is not a fair postulation. The roads and bridges were built by the government using tax dollars collected from the citizens. It is safe to assume that most business owners worked as employees for a few years and paid taxes on those wages. In this case, they've already paid for the roads. Once the businesses open, they pay taxes and the government uses this money to pay for necessary services such as police and fire. So, the businesses are getting benefits from the government but they are already paying for them. After all the bills are paid, including taxes, the owner gets the profits. They are then taxed on this income. Was President Obama saying that after all of the business expenses and income taxes the wealthy had paid, they still had not paid enough to cover the services rendered by the government? This is completely illogical. Even if you want to stretch the point and say that businesses do use slightly more of the roads than the rest of us to get products delivered and things of that nature, wouldn't the vendors who they buy their products from and the carriers they use for deliveries be paying taxes as well? Exactly how much do these roads and bridges cost?

In all of the posturing on both sides, there was a race to analyze the comments. I read articles and watched pundits from both sides and tried to find the truth somewhere in the middle. I stumbled upon an article from the *Huffington Post* written by Michael Smerconish, a Liberal columnist and radio talk show host. In the article, he posited that Obama was right and was just taken out of context. He referenced a statement made by Elizabeth Warren in August of 2011 in which she defended the Liberal economic theory and became a YouTube sensation.

"Speaking in Andover, Massachusetts, Elizabeth Warren said, 'You built a factory out there? Good for you,' and then she went on to say, 'But I want to be clear: You moved your goods to market on the roads the rest of us paid for; you hired workers the rest of us paid to educate; you were safe in your factory because of police forces and fire forces that the rest of us paid for. You didn't have to worry that marauding bands would come and seize everything at your factory, and hire someone to protect against this, because of the work the rest of us did.' "

Smerconish went on to write, "As for the tax implications, Warren said, 'Now look, you built a factory and it turned into something terrific, or a great idea? God bless. Keep a big hunk of it. But part of the underlying social contract is you take a hunk of that and pay forward for the next kid who comes along.' The crowd enthusiastically applauded."

Here again, the assumption is that the businessman just sprang up from nowhere, never paying taxes before. So when Warren speaks of "...the work the rest of us did," she'd have to include the businessman in that group. Smerconish was trying to say that Obama had the proper intent, but that he just didn't word it properly. He thinks that Warren did a better job of making the case as evidenced by the following, "Ten months ago, upon watching the clip, I said on the radio that, unlike President Obama, Warren had found her voice with a finely honed message for the middle class. While the size of the 'hunk' that should be paid 'forward for the next kid' is debatable, her underlying premise was solid."[93]

Mr. Smerconish is completely wrong. Not about the premise; I've already established that it is illogical, and it's troubling that someone would call her premise "solid". He's wrong in his assertion that Warren's comments were better than Obama's. Obama did a masterful job based on what I believe he was trying to do. He was trying to say the same thing Warren said without having it come off so one-sided. Warren basically said, "You made some money; now keep a chunk but give us an equal chunk." Obama smoothed those comments into, "You had help, so you should help those who helped you." We will find later that in most cases those successful businessmen not only do give back to those who helped them, but they give quite a bit more than people would expect.

It is unfortunate that this is how we get our news now. The art of just reporting facts and letting people decide is virtually gone. I still watch the news, but it has primarily become a topic source for me. They show a story, and if I'm interested, I go and do research. This actually scares me since such a small number of people even bother. Roughly 120 million people voted in the 2012 presidential election. Of them, I would guess that about 10% did any detailed research. What's more disappointing is that of that 10%, most people only researched sites that are slanted toward their views. Without both sides, what were they truly gaining? This means that the number of voters who had a true knowledge of where our politicians stood and a strong grasp of the issues was probably around 2% of the total electorate.

Party Misconceptions

I n addition to the lies and confusion created by politicians, there are general misconceptions about both parties that are common and tend to influence how people vote. It is a bad idea to take these misconceptions and assume a politician's views on an issue based on party affiliation. Most issues are too complex to simplify, and not all politicians agree with the party line on every issue. Taking these misconceptions at face value leads to the false assumptions and the stereotypes discussed earlier about race, gender, and other groups.

I've heard a lot of people say, "I'm an Independent, but I can't trust the Republicans because they are all multi-millionaires and cannot relate to the rest of us." We've also heard a lot about the "War on Women" within the Republican Party, and it is common knowledge that the vast majority of Blacks vote Democrat because they believe Republicans are racist. There are also misconceptions about the Democrats. These misconceptions are all detrimental to our process, as both parties exaggerate them to affect how people vote. Here is a brief summary of some common misconceptions about both parties:

The Democrats:
Care more about minorities
Care more about the poor
Are soft on national security
Are anti-business
Are anti-religion

The Republicans:
Are all racists
Are all rich White men
Constantly get us into wars
Try to control social issues
Are all religious zealots

These misconceptions need to be addressed using logic in order to dispel them. Democrats reading this book will say that only addressing the misconceptions of one party is unfair and biased. First, it needs to be said that none of these misconceptions are true. Though they may apply to some individuals in the parties, they do not represent the majority of either party. My goal is to be fair, but I decided to focus on the misconceptions about Republican's for two reasons.

The first is that as you look at the misconceptions of both parties, you notice that the misconceptions about Republicans are all negative while misconceptions about Democrats are split. This means that in the rhetoric department, the Democrats have a built-in advantage. Though both parties unfairly manipulate these beliefs, there are some naturally accepted views about Democrats that are positive.

The more important reason to focus on the Republican's misconceptions goes back to the groups the book is targeted at,

Republicans and Blacks. The Republicans already know that all of these are false, even though they try to twist the ones about Democrats in their favor. As for Blacks, we tend to believe them all, except for the anti-religion one. This is interesting, because of the nine remaining, five are negative views about Republicans, while two are positive views about Democrats, and two are views that Republicans use to denigrate Democrats but most Blacks don't view as negatives. Many Blacks are happy believing that Democrats are anti-business and soft on national security. Unfortunately, these are not true.

Republicans are all racists

My views on racism have been explained in great detail, but it's necessary to make one more thing clear. If we throw out all logic, Black Democrats would still dispel their own myth about Republicans. As I stated earlier, the majority of Blacks believe that over 75% of all Whites are racist. Though I find this to be racist and no different than Whites believing that 75% of Black men are criminals, let's accept this premise for a moment. If roughly 48% of the population are Democrats and 48% are Republicans, factoring in Independents, it bears the question, how can all Republicans be racist and 75% of all Whites be racist, yet no White Democrats are racist? At the very least, this will make half the White Democrats racists, yet you never hear racist allegations about them.

While there is no real indication that there are more racist politicians in one party than the other, it can be argued that the majority of White racists vote Republican. Like many other assumptions, this is not policy driven. If the virtual entirety of the Black community votes for Democrats, then these racists are simply voting against them. The Democrats have also done a great job of labeling Republicans as racists. So, if Blacks believe this and vote Democrat, isn't it logical to assume that White racists believe it and think they are voting for people who support their beliefs, even though there is no evidence that these racist beliefs are generally accepted among Republicans?

The real difference between the two parties when it comes to race is that the Democrats like to talk about what they want to do for specific groups, Blacks, women, Hispanics, etc., while the Republican say their plans are helpful to the entire country and believe that helping the majority will help everyone including people in all of these groups.

Neither party does a great job of addressing issues in the Black community, but only the Republicans are labeled as racists. The debate can be had about which party's policies are more beneficial, but when the Republicans argue in favor of policies that the Democrats don't believe in, instead of saying that the policies are wrong, they attack the intent. This is what I call, "The racism of disagreeing." Because of this, the Black community continues to suffer from the same problems all under Democratic policies — but they never question them.

To gain a broad spectrum of information, I watch a variety of news shows and listen to a lot of talk radio. While there are a few shows in my area that are considered Liberal, most are Conservative. I find this odd in an area that is predominately Liberal. When I tell my Liberal friends that I listen to talk radio, they say it's nothing but a bunch of Right-wing racists spewing hate about Democrats in general and Obama specifically. They call this proof that Conservatives are racist and say that their listeners are all racist Republicans. Logic proves otherwise. Take a look at this ranking of talk radio listenership conducted by *Talkers Magazine*:[94]

THE TOP TALK RADIO AUDIENCES

(Weekly Monday-Sunday cume estimates 6-plus in millions rounded off to the nearest .25 million based upon *TALKERS* magazine's analysis of a national sampling of Arbitron reports supported by other reliable indicators in rated and non-rated markets based on Spring 2012 data. This report is published quarterly.)

Radio Talk Show Host	Minimum Weekly Cume (millions)	Radio Talk Show Host	Minimum Weekly Cume (millions)
1. Rush Limbaugh	14.75+	8. Alan Colmes	3.25+
2. Sean Hannity	14.00+	Thom Hartmann	
		Rusty Humphries	
3. Michael Savage	8.75+	Dennis Miller	
4. Glenn Beck	8.25+	Stephanie Miller	
Mark Levin		Ed Schultz	
Dave Ramsey		9. Don Imus	2.25+
5. Neal Boortz	5.75+	Kim Komando	
Laura Ingraham		10. Hugh Hewitt	1.75+
6. Jim Bohannon	3.75+	Mancow	
Jerry Doyle		Todd Schnitt	
Mike Gallagher		Michael Smerconish	
Michael Medved		11. Lars Larson	1.50+
Doug Stephan		Dennis Prager	
7. Bill Bennett	3.50+	12. Warren Ballentine	1.00+
Clark Howard		Dr. Joy Browne	
George Noory		Gordon Deal	
		Bill Handel	
		Eric Harley &	
		Gary McNamara	
		Roger Hedgecock	
		Al Sharpton	

The numbers in The Top Talk Radio Audiences are estimates of national Arbitron numbers gathered directly by station reports and information provided by Arbitron and other sources as they relate to talk shows on news/talk-formatted radio stations. These figures are rough projections based upon a significant sample and do not represent exact Arbitron or any other ratings service totals.

Please credit *TALKERS* magazine if reproduced or cited. © 2012 Talk Media, Inc.

While there are shows from both sides, the Conservative shows dominate the ratings. Of the 37 shows that made the list, the top 5 (which actually includes 8 shows due to ties) has more listeners at 73.75 million than the other 29 shows combined at 70.25 million. Also, of the total list, only seven of the shows, totaling 16.75 million of the 144 million listeners, are considered Liberal talk shows. In contrast, shows that are considered Conservative or Libertarian represent 112.75 million of the 144 million listeners.

This doesn't count shows whose hosts don't label their party affiliation, such as Doug Stephan, Don Imus, as well as shows that don't have a political premise, such as Dave Ramsey (financial), Clark Howard (consumer finance), George Noory (paranormal), Kim Komando (computers), and Dr. Joy Browne (psychologist). This means that the first clearly Liberal show on the list is Alan Colmes, which is the 17th ranked show on the list.

If we take the Conservative listenership, 113 million listeners, and assume that 90% are Republicans, that would give us roughly 90 million listeners. If we account for repeated listenership (those listening to multiple shows), that would give us a total of over 60 million people. Isn't it logical to assume that these listeners are engaged and registered to vote? In 2008, 130 million people voted. Obama received 70 million votes while McCain only got 60 million. What are all these Conservative radio listeners doing? The 60 million talk radio listeners couldn't be more than half of the McCain voters. Doesn't this mean that many Conservatives cast their votes for Obama? With over 60 million racist Republicans ready to vote, how was Obama even elected?

The reason I mention this is because Democrats believe that the people who listen to these Conservative talk shows are closed-minded racists who are all Republicans. There is no way that these Conservative talk shows have so many engaged listeners and yet Obama won so handily. If it is true that most of these listeners are Conservatives, then doesn't this prove that Conservatives are more open-minded than Liberals believe?

Republican are all rich White men

We hear the argument regularly that Republicans are all rich White men. When this is challenged, many Democrats will amend the argument only by adding poor Whites that are racist and live in rural areas. Starting with the 'lack of diversity' argument, it is an example of circular reasoning. Republicans are rebuked for being the party for White men. However, many minorities and women, some of whom share their views on the issues, refuse to join the Republican Party because they believe they are racist. If the Republican Party is a majority of White men, it's because the minority groups won't join them and not because they are keeping them out.

As for the Republicans being rich, part of it has to do with the first argument. If the party is made up of a majority of White men, logic presumes they will have a higher median income than any other group, since men, in general, make more than women, and Whites also, on average, make more than minorities. They are also more likely to be married than Democrats, which lends itself to a two-income household.

This explains why, on average, they'd have more money, but it has nothing to do with the claim that they are all rich. Rich is a relative term, but the argument from Democrats is usually about millionaires and billionaires and not the middle class. This part is simply not true. We all hear about many wealthy people, and they tend to be Democrats and Republicans: the Koch brothers and Sheldon Adelson on the Right, and Warren Buffet and George Soros on the Left. There are many super-rich people on both sides. Many business leaders are assumed to be on the Right, while all of Hollywood is assumed to be on the Left. Let's call that a wash. Next, I decided to look inside our government. This is where things get interesting.

With the constant claims from the Democrats that Republicans are evil wealthy people with no empathy for those less fortunate and are so rich that they are out of touch, imagine my surprise when I looked at our super rich political leaders. Here's a list of politicians with a net worth of $10 million or more followed by the salaries of Congress as well as the president and vice-president:[95]

Wealthiest Political Leaders

Name	Est. Net worth to nearest million
Michael Bloomberg (I-NY)	19,500
Winthrop Rockefeller (D-AR)	1,200
Tony Sanchez (D-TX)	500
Amo Houghton (R-NY)	475
Jon Corzine (D-NJ)	300
Michael McCaul (R-Texas)	294
Darrell Issa (R-CA)	220
Jane Harman (D-CA)	200
John Kerry (D-Mass)	194
Jared Polis (D-CO)	160
Bob Corker (R-TN)	104
Rick Scott (R-FL)	103
Bill and Hillary Clinton (D-NY)	102
Alan Grayson (D-FL)	100
Jay Rockefeller (D-WV)	86
Mark Warner (D-VA)	76
Frank R. Lautenberg (D-NJ)	55
Richard Blumenthal (D-Conn)	53
Vernon Buchanan (R-FL)	45
Dianne Feinstein (D-CA)	45
Nancy Pelosi (D-CA)	35
Barack Obama (D-IL)	12
Herb Kohl (D-WI)	10

Salaries
Political Leaders
(annual pay as of 2012)

Rank and File members	$ 174,000
Senate Leadership	
Majority Party Leader	$ 193,400
Minority Party Leader	$ 193,400
House Leadership	
Speaker of the House	$ 223,500
Majority Leader	$ 193,400
Minority Leader	$ 193,400
President	$ 400,000
Vice President	$ 230,700

There are 22 politicians with a net worth greater than $10 million, and look, only six of them are Republicans. And while the U.S. median household income in 2011 was $50,054[97], the minimum yearly pay for a congressional member is $174,000 — nearly three and a half times that of the average household. The point here is — they're *all* rich.

We can go back and forth on whose policies work the best, but it is unfair to imply that one party is made up of wealthy plutocrats while the other party is made up of benevolent social workers with no interest in money. Are we supposed to believe that these wealthy Democrats didn't use the same tactics as the Republicans to make their fortunes? Some politicians fit these stereotypes, but for every rich Republican out to destroy the middle class, there's a crooked Democrat illegally using government funds for his own benefit or for the benefit of his friends (*Sorry if I sound bitter. I grew up in N.W. Indiana and have worked in Chicago for nearly 20 years, which is where I currently live. I've seen too many politicians go to jail and too much money disappear. See appendix 1 below.*).

The attacks Romney received during the campaign were illogical. If Romney hated women and minorities so much, then why would he run for president? He's already rich. He could easily just relax and make his money. Do the Democrats really want us to think he was putting himself and his family through this scrutiny just to win the opportunity to oppress people? Even if you buy the argument that wealthy people are all evil, don't they eventually tend to end their lives giving back? Just take a look at Andrew Carnegie and John D. Rockefeller.

While both were tough businessmen who tried to monopolize their industries, often on the backs of others, they gave hundreds of millions of dollars to charity. They both believed that it was the duty of the wealthy to use their knowledge, expertise, connections, and money to help others. Perhaps Mitt had reached the point in his life where he was focused on giving back.

Republicans want to control social issues

At the Democratic National Convention, we heard speaker after speaker talk about the implied "War on Women" and how the election of a Republican president would end the rights of all women. Whether it was Nancy Keenan, the 'House Women', Maria Ciano, or Sandra Fluke, they all came out and attacked the Romney campaign and Conservatives for being women haters who needed to be stopped.[98] This was designed to get women who may be undecided to vote for Obama over Romney. The women's issues that were being discussed were reproductive rights, birth control, and equal pay for women, as well as taxpayer funding for Planned Parenthood. The implication was that if women want to maintain control of their bodies, then they must vote for Obama. Diana DeGette, U.S. Representative for Colorado's 1st district, even went so far as to say that the Republicans wanted to make women, "2nd class citizens again." Some Liberals even said that they thought Mitt would be a more effective president but that they couldn't vote for him because he's a Republican and he wants to end abortion. Their arguments were extreme, and again, not based on logic.

It implied that as Conservatives we are all Neanderthals with God complexes. Let's pause a moment for a quick education. I will attest that of the people who are pro-life, there are far more Republicans than Democrats. This in no way means that they are trying to control anyone's body. In fact, much of the Black community is pro-life. There are also a large number of fiscal Republicans who are more Liberal on social issues. When speaking of social issues, the Democrats always use the president's ability to appoint Supreme Court justices as an important reason to vote for the Democratic candidate. They say that if Republicans are allowed to nominate justices, their evil Right-wing ways would overtake the country and women and minorities would lose their rights. There is no doubt that this type of rhetoric can sway voters, but it is not based in fact nor is it a logical way of seeing things. Here are some facts about the Supreme Court.

Since 1949, only one chief justice, Fred Vinson, was appointed by a Democrat. In fact, since Lincoln made his first appointment to the court in 1862, we've only had 3 chief justices appointed by Democrats. Also, of the 79 justices appointed in that timeframe, 52 were appointed by Republicans and 27 by Democrats. This means that Republican-appointed judges led the court when the following groundbreaking cases were decided:

Brown v. Board of Education (Unanimous)
Roe v. Wade – 7-2 (dissent, 1 R, 1 D)
Miranda v. Arizona – 5-4 (dissent, 2 R, 2 D)
Lawrence v. Texas – 6-3 (dissent, all R,
but 7 of the nine justices were Republicans)
Planned Parenthood v. Casey (Plurality)

The Roe v. Wade decision was issued in 1973.[99] Since the decision, we've had eight presidents, counting Nixon who was president at the time of the decision, five Republicans and three Democrats. Even though most of the Republican presidents opposed abortion, there was never any talk about them trying to reverse the law. Although some tried to implement provisions such as spousal and parental notifications, or limitations on late term and partial-birth abortions, this can hardly be considered a reversal of the law.

Where is all of the legislation that proves they are trying to take away rights, or the activist justices who want to control social issues from the bench? The same can be said about the birth control issue. They painted the picture that Republicans were trying to ban birth control when the argument was actually focused on whether religious institutions should be forced to cover birth control in their health plans or whether or not it should be paid for by taxpayers.

Again, the argument that Republicans were trying to ban birth control or control women's bodies was drastically overstated.

When it comes to equal pay, women and minorities have been fighting for equality for years. If we are going to approach this logically, then we must first admit that there is not an equal pay issue until the employer systematically pays women or minorities less than their male or White counterparts. This is a problem, but placing the blame for this at the feet of the Republicans is like saying all business owners and hiring managers are Republicans. Logically, there has to be some cases where the Democrat boss is discriminating against his minority or female employees.

I also believe the comments made about the "implied" Republican "War on Women" were sexist. This is why they had women make the arguments. Although they did a great job of getting people fired up, the entire premise was exaggerated. They acted as if women couldn't speak for themselves or defend themselves so they needed the benevolent Democrats to save them. Aren't those views sexist? Women make up 50% of the population. Even if the evil Republicans were trying to impose strict laws against abortion or any other issue specifically affecting women, all that the women would have to do is vote against it. If it was so egregious, they would have over 90% of the female vote, and they would easily get at least 30% of men to join them. That would be more than enough to knock down any attempt to limit women's rights. The bottom line is; if they want to truly address these social issues, then they have to accept the fact that voting for a particular party will not solve them.

Republicans are all religious zealots

It is often said that Republicans are a bunch of religious zealots. The graphic shown below was taken from a Gallop poll on church attendance by party affiliation, and the results are fascinating. They actually dispel both the myth that Republicans are all zealots and the myth that Democrats are all secular. The totals are aggregate totals from three years of surveys.

Church Attendance, by Party ID and Race

Percentage who attend weekly/almost weekly/monthly

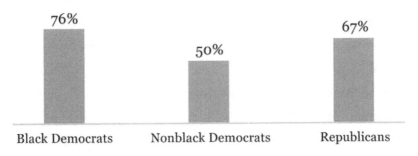

Frank Newport, "Blacks as Conservative as Republicans on Some Moral Issues", Gallop, 12/3/08

The first thing we notice is that at 67% for Republicans, the church attendance is high but not so high that it indicates an anomaly from society. Next, at 50%, the number for non-Black Democrats doesn't indicate a majority of secularists. The most telling stat, however, is the 76% for Black Democrats. The fact that their church attendance is even higher than that of Republicans shows that they tend to agree with Republicans on some of the social issues, and it shows that Republicans aren't that extreme in their religious views.

Since we will all agree that Blacks are overwhelmingly Democrats, we can combine the Black and non-Black Democrat numbers to guess the overall Democrat number for church attendance. Blacks are about 13% of the population, so since half of the population is Democrats, and we can put all the Blacks in with them, then they should total around 26% of the Democrats. Even if you take a Conservative number like 20%, that would add 15% to the non-Black total, making the overall totals 65% Democrat and 67% Republican — hardly an extreme difference.

It is also unfair to assume that because someone is an evangelical that he is prone to push his views on others. There are definitely some fanatics on both sides, but they are obviously in the minority. When a Right wing-nut makes some insane comment, it gets a lot of press but doesn't fairly represent all Republicans any more than a Left wing-nut represents all of the Democratic Party. In either instance, it is wrong to do anything more than call it what it is — a fanatic being himself.

Republicans constantly get us into wars

This is the last one and the one that I personally believed of the five misconceptions we are discussing. It's the one about Republicans being warmongers. So I drank the Kool-Aid, and how can you blame me? First of all, with the development of advanced weaponry as well as increased media coverage following Vietnam, the way we fight wars has been forever changed. Although this greatly improved our way of life during wartime, it changed our view on war and the military. In World War II, everybody knew someone who was in the war. There was virtually no unemployment with everyone who was not deployed working in factories to manufacture goods for the war. Coupling this with the propaganda images showing the military in a positive light, it's no wonder that morale was high, but Vietnam changed all that. The war was long; many didn't believe we should be there, and there were lots of negative stories about our troops. There was also constant news coverage showing terrible images from the front lines. The result was a hugely unpopular war, and military personnel decried the war when they returned.

I was born in the early seventies, so I missed all of that. The first mention of war I remember had nothing to do with an actual war; it was the money to be spent on defense that was being discussed. Reagan was president and wanted to increase defense spending. We were in the middle of the Cold War, and he felt that we needed to negotiate from a position of strength. Reagan wanted to fund missile defense, develop advanced weaponry, and upgrade the military. He also supported funding and assisting opposition to Communist foreign leaderships, which led to the Iran-Contra Affair.

Since the end of the Cold War, we continue to have the largest and most capable military in the world in addition to the most nuclear weapons. Democrats have made several attempts to cut defense spending but always with much opposition from Republicans. In this same time frame we've had a few conflicts, but the three wars we were taken into were all under Republican leadership, the Gulf War, Iraq, and Afghanistan. Taking all of this in its entirety, it's hard to deny the warmonger argument on the surface. But, as usual, using logic gets you different results.

As far as the spending goes, there is no doubt that the Republicans have been reluctant to cut the defense budget. This has more to do with how the military is evaluated and managed than it has with their desire to keep us at war. This leaves us with the actual conflicts. Many people object to these conflicts because they don't believe we should be in these countries in the first place. They would have to concede, however, that if a conflict cannot be avoided, we'd rather have it take place on foreign soil than here. I'm sure they would prefer not having conflicts at all, but the events on 9/11/01 showed that this isn't always possible. And with the exception of a small group such as Ron Paul (who's more Libertarian but ran as a Republican candidate for president) and Dennis Kucinich, very few politicians on either side seemed to be anti-war, in the beginning. Some politicians may argue about tactics, such as should we go to Iraq or Afghanistan, the number of troops we should send, whether we should get UN approval, etc., but very few of them are as anti-war as many Americans want them to be, Democrat or Republican.

In fact, the same three people we were dealing with throughout George W. Bush's presidency and much of Obama's, we were dealing with in the '80s and '90s. Reagan bombed Gaddafi, George HW Bush bombed Saddam Hussein, and Clinton went after Osama Bin Laden. And let's be clear, every time we were attacked by an outside entity, we retaliated. It never mattered which party was in power. That being a given, let's look at all the major conflicts and wars that the U.S. has been involved in since we've had the two party system and which party was in power.

War/Conflict	President	Party
Civil war	Lincoln	R*
Spanish American War	McKinley	R
Philippine War	McKinley	R
Mexican Occupation/Border Wars	Taft/Wilson	Split
WWI	Wilson	D
Russian Revolution	Wilson	D
Korea	Truman	D
WWII	FDR	D
Bay of Pigs/Cuban missile crisis	Kennedy	D
Vietnam	Eisenhower/LBJ	Split
Dominican Republic	LBJ	D
Lebanon	Reagan	R
Grenada	Reagan	R
Panama	Bush I	R
Gulf War	Bush I	R
Somalia	Clinton	D
Bosnia	Clinton	D
Kosovo	Clinton	D
Iraq	Bush II	R
Afghanistan	Bush II/Obama	R

As you can see, Democrats have gotten us into as many conflicts as have Republicans. Each conflict had its own specific situations, so it's hard to say which ones were right and which ones were wrong, but it can be argued that we were driven into the worst of them by Democrats. We can blame the current wars on Bush, but the Civil War was caused by the Democrats threatening secession. World War I was Wilson, while World War II was FDR, and the Bay of Pigs failure was Kennedy. Vietnam is a much more complicated conflict to delineate. Though U.S. involvement in Vietnam officially started under Eisenhower, Truman had been involved supplying military aid and assistance to the French Army nearly three years prior to Eisenhower's election.[100]U.S. involvement increased slightly under Kennedy, but the surge in Vietnam was implemented by Johnson, and Nixon executed the withdrawal. The Vietnam War was led by several commanders from both parties and has to be considered at best a push.

In addition, with President Obama increasing troops in Afghanistan, approving drone attacks, killing Bin Laden, and toppling Gaddafi, we can't really say he's all about peace. I'm not knocking him for much of it, but I just think Democrats are being hypocrites. They are essentially saying war is bad and we should stay out of other countries — unless a Democrat leads us there. Whatever you believe, there's no way to logically say that Republicans are warmongers. And as for the one time I believed in a stereotype without investigating, I stand corrected.

While all of these misconceptions are wrong and cannot be applied to the majority of either party, they have a disproportionately negative effect on Republicans. This is due to one basic premise: Republicans believe the Democrats are wrong, while Democrats believe the Republicans are bad people. This is telling, because those who say they are the most tolerant tend to be the most judgmental.

127

Who is the
Middle Class?

Turn on the news on any given day and you will hear talk about the middle class. Either there's a Republican pundit frantically stating that the Obama administration is destroying the middle class or a Democratic pundit warning us that the Republicans have declared a war on the middle class.[101] This is a great example of the lies we've discussed. The accuracy of the accusation is not important. We've already established that much of what we hear is an exaggeration of the truth, if not an outright lie. What is important is *why* there's such a push to make the middle class feel as if they are under attack.

The problem with this hard-fought battle to protect the middle class is that no one really knows who they're addressing. If you ask two average American households with different incomes what group they belong to, there's a good chance they will both say middle class even though their financial situations couldn't be more different. The fact is that the overwhelming majority of Americans consider themselves to be middle class. For example, a family of three living on $30,000 per year will likely say they are middle class, but so will a family of three making $75,000. If you ask another family of three, they may tell you they are poor; which is the same answer a family of three living on $50,000 may give you. Why is it so hard to determine who is actually in the middle class?[102]

The biggest reason no one can solidify who is in the middle class and why so many families consider themselves middle class regardless of their household income is that most of us don't really use income as the determining factor. The government can only look at hard data when creating its reports on household income. This includes factors such as race, sex, number of people in the household, and other measurable criteria. Unfortunately, this information is limiting because people don't base their social class by this data. Their values and lifestyles are more of a determining factor to the class they associate with than their income. These things cannot be measured by census data; therefore, there is a disconnect between those who the government considers to be middle class and those who believe they are part of the middle class.

When most people say they are middle class, they consider their beliefs, how they live, and their overall financial situation more than the actual amount on their paychecks or in their bank accounts. This is how families with vastly different incomes can feel the same about their social class. When you ask middle-class families what makes them middle class, they will say things that are loosely tied to money but not a specific amount. For example, most would say they get up every day and work hard for their money. They were not born with wealth and have no one to fall back on. Financially, they make enough money to stay current on their bills but not enough to build enough savings or to be worry free. They have to consider how to pay for emergencies

130

or large purchases, and they have some amount of debt. They also strive to improve their financial situations, believe in helping those less fortunate than they, and they frown upon those who take advantage of the system. They tend to have a strong sense of community and family and are thankful for what they have.

Looking at these views, one can understand why these families have so much in common even with such a wide income range. Most can relate to having a demanding job and working hard for their pay regardless of how much they make. There are many financially successful people who come from poor families or are the first in their families to go to college. In the example of the two families above, they can both be living in a similar manner; one just has more money with which to work. One family rents a two-bedroom apartment, while the other owns a house. One family has an older car that they own outright, while the other family has a newer car and pays a car note. One family has occasional get-togethers and they order takeout, while the other family dines out or goes to an occasional concert. The important thing is that at the end of the month they both can pay their bills and feel that they have just enough to enjoy themselves. They are better off than many families, but neither could survive more than a couple of months if they suffered a loss of income, so they aren't as 'comfortable' as are the wealthy.

The situation described above is experienced by the majority of the country, even though they have varying incomes. This alone makes it nearly impossible to definitively place people in a certain social class. However, even if we focus solely on income, we run into problems determining who should be placed within the middle class. This is because when all things seem to be equal, further examination shows that they can be very different. Even when looking at families with the same number of people in the household and the same income, there are factors that drastically affect how they actually live. While there are myriad situations that can affect how household income is dispersed, here are some of the most common.

The number of income earners in the household is a key factor in determining how household income is spent. As most will agree, the cost of childcare is a large percentage of the household expenses. For families with one income, there can be a considerable savings in this category if the other parent stays home to take on this responsibility. There are also other cost savings when one parent stays at home. When both parents work, they may order carryout dinners a little more often, and they will both most likely buy lunch when they are working. They also have other costs, such as dry cleaning and a second car, and that could add to their expenses.

Obviously, the previous paragraph assumes that the household is made up of a couple with a child. This is not always the case, so it is important to mention that married couples are far more likely to consider themselves middle class than single parents. Single-parent households generally have a more difficult time due to the nature of the family makeup, and since we are focusing on three person households for the consistency of these comparisons, that change in dynamics will have a great impact on the family income because there will be two children instead of one and only one wage earner. Therefore, we will continue under the assumption that there are two adults in the household for the remainder of this comparison.

Where a family lives can also dictate how far their money can go. The census stats draw the poverty line at around $19,000. It is slightly higher for Alaska and Hawaii. After that, there is no real distinction. However, we all know that $50,000 in NYC is completely different from $50,000 in Dalhart, Texas where I spent my summers as a child. The cost of living is also different when comparing rural areas to urban areas. Needless to say, poor, middle class, and rich are situational distinctions.

Another factor that the census data cannot consider is how people handle their finances. It is often said that most Americans live beyond their means. Does this cause some people to feel poor, while their income may put them in the middle class? What about the other way around? If a family has less income but does a better job at managing it, will they still consider themselves middle class in spite of the income?

In 2000, I lost my job and was deciding what I wanted to do next. I had been thinking about opening my own business for a while and thought this would be a good time to focus on that. Instead of looking for full-time work, I took a part-time job so I'd have time to work on my business plan. Since I knew I'd be making considerably less money, I made it a point to cut my expenses. I moved into an apartment that was not in the best neighborhood, but the rent was only $325 per month. I then cut out most of my discretionary spending. Although I made less than half of what I was making when employed full time, I was able to keep current on my bills and save a little of my income. I'm not sure if I would have called myself middle class back then, but I definitely would not have said I was poor.

This brings up another point that goes beyond actual income. People have a negative view of being poor, but not in the sense that they put down those who are poor; they simply view being poor as a situation you need help to get out of. Because of this, they are more likely to say they are middle class than claim to be part of the proletariat. Many also hear "poor" and think of people getting government assistance or begging for help; therefore, no matter what their income, they feel that if they aren't getting government assistance and they aren't begging, then they aren't poor.

Therefore, when politicians speak of the middle class, who they are addressing and what they are trying to accomplish depends on which party they represent. They look at the census data and see what percentage of households fall into each quintile. However, they also see all the polls and surveys that say most Americans relate to the middle class. They use this information to direct the attacks on their opponents to the one segment of the populations most people feel they belong to — the middle class. When we hear about some terrible thing a politician is doing to hurt the middle class, we feel that we are the ones threatened. So, depending on who we believe, we assume that the other party is wrong.

Republicans use this as an opportunity to attack Democrats. President Obama campaigns on the premise that we need to tax the rich more to help pay the country's bills. So, when he says they need to pay their fair share, Republicans don't argue that it's unfair to tax them more. What they argue is that Obama doesn't understand what rich is and really intends to tax the middle class. They know that many people make more than $250,000 but make far less than a million dollars and consider themselves to be middle class. So, Republicans saying that Obama counts them in with millionaires and billionaires will resonate with many of them.

The Democrats, on the other hand, want you to believe that the Republicans only care about the rich, and the tax cuts they propose will help them while hurting the middle class. Since the economy is struggling and so many people are hurting, they know that helping the rich just seems elitist and out of touch. Romney insists that he wants to lower tax rates across the board, while Obama wants to raise taxes.

Again, like most issues, both groups are exaggerating the truth in their attacks. However, the point here is that they are both capitalizing on our view of what being middle class is. If you agree with the Republicans, then you are afraid that Obama is trying to redistribute wealth at the expense of the middle class. If you agree with the Democrats, then you are afraid that Romney is trying to help the rich on the backs of the middle class. Neither argument is actually true, but they hope that using the term 'middle class' will get the majority of the voting populous to take notice. That being said, in spite of all the rhetoric on both sides, neither party is doing a great job at helping the middle class — whoever *they* are.

The Truth About the One Percent

These promises to, and fervent fights about, the middle class have become business as usual for politicians, and this year's presidential campaign was no different. Every candidate continued to pander to the middle class to gain votes; however, the attacks on the rich greatly increased. Don't get me wrong; there have always been attacks on the rich, but now these attacks seem even more vicious.

After the stock market collapsed in 2008, when many lost their jobs and savings, there seemed to be a more hostile divide between the "Haves" and the "Have nots". We started to hear about the Occupy Wall Street Movement, which, on the surface, claimed to be a group dedicated to fight for the 99% and to stop the favoritism and unfair practices of the 1%.[103] They described the 1% as the millionaires and billionaires who were being bailed out by the government, shirking their tax liabilities, and making money in the recession, when many of us were losing our homes and our savings.

The top 1% earn on average about $340,000 per year.[104] Although they make far more than the average American, they are far from the evil wealthy people we envision when we think of the so-called 1%. Many of them, contrary to the Republican's assertion, are not business owners. They are employees at some of the same large businesses where many of us work. They make more money because of their advanced education, specialized skills, or business experience. Their household incomes are further inflated by the fact that they are more likely to be married and are often married to another professional. Most of these earners are also a little older and have moved up within their companies while gaining more experience and responsibility, hence, higher pay.

Some of the 1% are indeed small business owners. However, many have really small businesses, with typically only a small number of employees outside of family members. They have to be there day in and day out for the business to function. They may be in the top 1% of income earners, but they are not the 1% who concern the Occupy protesters. They didn't get bailed out; instead, they lost much of their retirement funds, and many of them went out of business.

As for the real object of the Occupy Movement's ire, these are the true millionaires and billionaires. This is the flaw in the Occupy Movement's attacks. While the 1% sounds nice, millionaires are a much smaller percent of the population, about 0.1%. Billionaires are even rarer at around 400 people in the US.[105] We hear this and think that these people are making billions in income every year, but this value is based on net worth, not actual income. Most of their net worth comes from investments in the stock market, real estate, and businesses. Other billionaires have created some new

138

innovation or product and sold their idea to a larger company. They are the hedge fund managers, Fortune 500 CEOs, professional athletes, and much of Hollywood. However they achieved it, these people control the majority of the wealth and pay the majority of the taxes in the U.S.

Those who say that the rich should pay more taxes are dismissed by Republicans as naïve people who don't understand the economy or jealous people who only want to punish success. While some may fall into this category, this isn't the case for the majority of them. There is definitely a large percentage of the population who don't know how much in taxes the rich pay. It's not because it hasn't been repeated over and over; it's because we are generally selfish and focused on our own situations. Many will hear the statistics and say, "They're rich, so they can afford it." Since it doesn't affect them, they have no reason to take time to think about whether it's fair or not. This is why as people make more money they tend to wonder more and more about how much they're being taxed and where the money is going.

As far as jealousy being the cause of animosity toward the rich, I think many people wish they were rich but don't go so far as being jealous. In fact, the behavior of most Americans shows that we admire those who have achieved success. This explains our fascination with celebrities, business leaders, and some politicians. If this is the case for most Americans, what explains the vitriolic attacks on the rich?

For most people, it's not how rich a person is that creates hostility; it's how they got rich or, more accurately, the perception of how they got rich. If a person's wealth was attained through hard work, creativity, or even luck, we tend to be okay with it. If,

139

however, the perception is that their wealth was gained through unscrupulous dealings or through inheritance, then it is less accepted.

When we hear a story about someone who started from nothing and after working hard for years became rich, we applaud him or her. Most of us think of this as living the American Dream. We like our celebrities. They entertain us and tend to be glamorous and cool, so we live vicariously through them; however, we don't tend to admire them unless they have a particularly interesting story or they lead an admirable life outside the spotlight. For example, we find many celebrities interesting to watch, but we admire celebrities such as George Clooney, Brad Pitt, and Gary Sinise for the contributions they make outside of Hollywood.

Business leaders are different; they tend to be admired more because they were able to create something we can see. They invented something that made our lives easier or they improved processes that already existed. Many had ideas we wish we had thought of, while others created things we don't even understand. In either case, these businesses created jobs and helped stimulate the economy.

The problem arises when some leaders take shortcuts to achieve success. They cut corners on their products, mislead their customers, and sometimes break the law. While this is a small percentage of businesses, when these stories come out, it reflects poorly on other businesses. So, when some companies were found to be falsifying financial reports, all companies were scrutinized. This is how Sarbanes-Oxley was passed.[106] A problem is found in a small percentage of businesses, albeit a devastating problem, and new regulation is presented to try to control all businesses. The same goes for the banking industry.

When the housing collapse was linked to unscrupulous banking practices, the government swooped in with new regulations. This is an emotional reaction to do something because it feels right. While many people react in this manner, it is not the way the government should operate. Sometimes it is necessary to create new regulations, but many times the proper regulations are already in place and we just need officials to enforce them. Creating new regulations is costly for the government to manage and for businesses to follow. Since the primary goal of a business is to make a profit, they pass these additional costs on to the consumer. We are now being charged an inflated price for their goods and services, or, worse yet, companies lay off employees in an attempt to cut costs.

There is one other characteristic of the rich we tend not to admire as much: people who inherit their wealth. Many people don't have the same respect for those who were born with a silver spoon in their mouths as they have for those who started out poor. The perception is that they didn't earn what they got and started with an unfair advantage. It is probably derived from jealousy. People may think that they would have the same level of success if they were given these advantages. The interesting thing here is how we decide who earned their money and who is a spoiled rich kid. Let's look at two wealthy families and compare how they are perceived, the Kennedys and the Romneys.

Joe Kennedy grew up in an upper-middle-class family. Even though all four of his grandparents had emigrated from Ireland to escape the famine, by the time Joe was a young boy, his father was successful and had gained some prominence as a community leader and ward boss. Joe attended Harvard University and started working in the banking industry.[107] He made most of his fortune through investments in both the stock market and real estate. Sometimes rumored to be involved in nefarious activities, including activities that led to the stock market crash of 1929, Kennedy gained tremendous wealth, and by the late 1950s, he had an estimated net worth of $400 million (roughly $3B today).[108] FDR later appointed him the first chairman of the SEC.[109]

The family continued the legacy he started. Many of his descendants attended Harvard, following in his footsteps. Since 1960, the family boasts a U.S. President, an Attorney General, two U.S. Senators, two U.S. Ambassadors, two members of Congress, the founder of the Special Olympics, and several powerful attorneys, business leaders, and journalists. They also have several foundations that donate millions of dollars to charitable causes.[110]

George Romney was born in Mexico to parents living in Mormon colonies there.[111] Having been displaced by the Mexican Revolution, they moved several times, trying to improve their circumstances.[112] Whenever his father's success faltered, they would move again. George spent most of his childhood poor and moving between Idaho and Utah. He worked odd jobs and went to college part-time. He attended several colleges but never finished. George eventually moved to DC to work as a lobbyist for the automotive industry.[113] He ended up in Michigan working his way up to CEO of American Motors Corporation.[114] After working to build up the success of the company and drastically increasing the value of the company, he became a millionaire by way of his stock options. He did all this while maintaining a significant role in his church.

After conquering the business world, George Romney left to pursue a career in politics and became Governor of Michigan in 1963. He was a strong supporter of the Civil Rights Movement, and in his first State of the Union Address, he said, "Michigan's most urgent human rights problem is racial discrimination — in housing, public accommodations, education, administration of justice, and employment.[115] He was considered a moderate Republican and opposed Barry Goldwater's candidacy in the 1964 presidential election.

George Romney would make civil rights a focus during his entire political career. He created Michigan's first Civil Rights Commission and marched in Detroit to support the Selma, Alabama March. In fact, this turned out to be one of the few times he went against his church, vowing to continue his efforts toward civil rights in spite of the church not supporting it and disallowing Blacks from holding positions in the priesthood.[116] Because of his stance on civil rights, George Romney received over 30% of the Black vote in his last election as Michigan's Governor, an impressive accomplishment for a Republican in 1966.[117]

Mitt Romney received an MBA and Law degree from Harvard University and went to work at Boston Consulting Group. He later joined Bain and Company, becoming a vice president after just over one year. He eventually left Bain and Company to co-found Bain Capital. Working as a venture capitalist, he focused on start-ups and helped them grow. Later, he moved away from start-ups and started to focus on restructuring existing companies that were struggling, making them more solvent and then selling them for a profit. This made him millions. He took a break from Bain to work as CEO of the Winter Olympics in Salt Lake City. After the success of the Olympics, he sold his share of Bain and went into public service, running for the Senate and later becoming Governor of Massachusetts to equal his father's accomplishments.

These are two examples of very successful families. They worked hard, took advantage of their opportunities, and had competitive drives that allowed them to succeed. After conquering the business world, both families pursued public service to give back more than they could financially to the country that had been so good to them.

Based on the backgrounds described, if you had to guess which family was admired most, you'd probably say the Romney family. George Romney started off poor and didn't finish college. He made his wealth in investments but got his success in business, turning around an auto company. Though Mitt was a venture capitalist, he successfully built a business. He also invested millions in start-ups and in growing companies that he helped guide to success.

Joe Kennedy had a more stable upbringing than George Romney and attended Harvard. He worked in the 'evil' banking industry and made his money almost exclusively through investments. He was rumored to have at best been involved in insider trading and at worst been guilty of bootlegging and trying to fix his son's presidential election. So why are the Kennedys adored while Mitt Romney was painted in this year's election as an evil rich person who only cares about money. This was widely believed in spite of the fact that he and his father always maintained strict ties to their church. The only plausible explanation would have to be political affiliation. There is really no other difference. If you make millions of dollars, then you most likely have a company investing your money. So millionaires across the board invest in blue chip companies and start-ups, and they invest in some companies who do most of their business in the U.S. as well as others who move their operations offshore. This is not a Democrat or Republican thing, yet wealthy Republicans are constantly questioned while wealthy Democrats get a pass. I simply want to see consistency. It is illogical to assume that all the honest businessmen are Democrats and all the crooks are Republicans. The lines have to become blurry somewhere.

Now that we have established who the wealthy are, it's important to address the taxation issue. I agree that we need to do what's best for the country, including raising taxes on the wealthiest Americans, if that *is* what's best. The problem is that it's not being proposed because it's the best plan; it's only being proposed because it sounds good. Also, the majority of people who agree with it do so because they are being selfish. If they aren't wealthy, then they don't care because it won't affect them. The moment it does affects them, they'll get upset. I have two simple reasons I believe tax hikes should be limited.

The first is that we have no evidence that they will work. Superfluous government spending is our real problem. We already know that the government devours money. The more tax revenue they take in, the more the government will spend. This eliminates the incentive to cut spending by shifting the focus. In addition, increasing taxes on the top one or two percent will not raise enough additional revenue. Even if the tax increase is agreed upon, much of the added revenue will be cut by adjustments made by the wealthy.

Businesses that are taxed will increase their prices to make up for the income losses. They may even downsize the business,

145

and that hurts even more people. When wealthy individuals are taxed more, they will take advantage of more loopholes, and if loopholes aren't available, they will spend less or invest less, which will negate some of the impact.

The second reason tax hikes should be limited is because the money belongs to the individuals who earn it and not the government. We all have varying levels of skills and talents, and we market those to determine how much we can make. If the market says our skills are valuable, we make a lot of money, but if not, we don't make as much. Whatever the market determines you are worth should be yours.

Very few people would have been able to create technology such as the iPod, mass produce the automobile as did Henry Ford, develop elegant cuisine as does Grant Achatz, or make successful music for fifty years as have the Rolling Stones. They all offered the public a product or service the public wanted and were willing to pay for, so why shouldn't they be rich? The government needs money to run, and we all have to, as President Obama insists, pay our fair share, but every American deserves to keep more than half of their pay. We all may be a little envious of the wealthy, but it doesn't entitle us to their money, and it surely is no reason to want to penalize them for being rich.

They won't say how much is enough, but I don't believe that anyone should have to pay more than 40% of their income to the government, including federal, state, and local taxes, as well as Social Security and all other taxes. Also, if a person lives in a state whose taxes are so high that it brings their total to over 40%, the federal government should credit them the balance. You have to admit that a 60/40 split of money that you earned is more than fair.

146

Speaking of the value of services, we are being overcharged by our politicians. Why should they be in the top 5% income bracket? We have political gridlock, an out of control deficit, and politicians fighting like children, yet, we still pay. Also, unlike the private sector, the market doesn't dictate what they make. They get to vote on their own salaries. The people governing our country should make a livable wage, otherwise we'd have even more theft, but they should not be as well off as they are. The average household in America makes around $50,000, while members of Congress make a minimum of $174,000.

We should demand that they pass a law that the salary of elected officials should be no higher than 20% above the average wage in their state. Why should they all make the same salary? The cost of living in Nebraska or Tennessee is nowhere near that of California, New York, or Hawaii. Limiting these salaries would also discourage career politicians. Most of these college-educated professionals would not stay in Congress for 30 years if it only paid $60,000. Limiting Congress alone to an average of $60,000 would save nearly $60 million, and this limit should not be for national politicians alone.

In Chicago, the average household makes $47,000 a year, while their 50 aldermen make an average of $112,345.[118] If you include mayors, governors, and other elected officials, it adds up to over a billion dollars wasted on inflated salaries. Cutting these salaries, as is the case with the tax hikes, won't really help the deficit, but it will be a symbolic gesture. Keep in mind that while the wealthy make their own money, we pay these officials with our taxes, the same taxes they want to raise. Cutting these salaries will also let those who are running for public office know that they can't get rich in public office. Many people support term limits for politicians, but we know this will never happen; in order to get it passed, the politicians themselves would have to vote for it. This is another reason to limit their salaries. If they cannot make the kind of money they are currently making, term limits will no longer be an issue. In the words of Mitt Romney, they would "self-deport" *themselves* out of office.

When talking about the 1%, the Republicans said that raising their taxes would hurt the economy because some of the 1% were small business owners and that the tax hike would slow their growth. This would undoubtedly happen in some cases, but is not nearly as prevalent as they made it out to be. While this is yet another case of politicians stretching the truth to get you to decide in their favor, this one is interesting. In this case they told a lie, because the truth would sound worse. What they would have said if they could be truthful is, "It's their money. They earned it legally and should be able to keep it." Saying this, however, would have been insensitive. People would have accused them of once more not caring about those in need — illogical.

Warren Buffet agreed with the "Buffet Rule", so many Democrats used his assertion as proof that the wealthy needed to pay more taxes. But wanting to keep the money you worked hard for is not uncaring or corrupt. In fact, the truth no one really talks about is that they all give millions of dollars to charity. There's always going to be some people who could probably give a little more than they do, but, as a whole, most wealthy people are very philanthropic. Obviously, they give more than the average person because they have so much more, but many of them pay more in taxes and give more to charity as a percentage of their annual incomes than the majority of Americans, and this is regardless of party affiliation.

Bill Gates,[119] Sheldon Adelson,[120] George Soros,[121] Dick Cheney,[122] and Mitt Romney[123] all give millions of dollars to charity every year. Think about it: When you take some of the richest families in American history — the Kennedys, Roosevelts, Rockefellers, and Carnegies, they have collectively given billions of dollars to charity. Raising taxes on the wealthy would be just a symbolic move. At the end of the day, their taxes could be raised as much as 4%, but they could just cut their charitable contributions by the same amount to offset their loss. Every action has a reaction.

My views on wealth and taxes are due to fairness and wanting to do what is right. If Congress votes to raise taxes on the top 2%, as President Obama campaigned on, it would have no effect on me. So, unlike the well-to-do Republican pundits on TV or the Conservative talk show hosts, you can't say that I might have selfish motives. The bottom line is that the wealthiest Americans are not as evil as some try to make them out to be, and there's no advantage to penalizing them. Also, it is illogical to believe that a wealthy Democrat is somehow different from a wealthy Republican. When people talk about the wealthy, party affiliation isn't a factor.

Lastly, the proponents of tax hikes should keep in mind the fact that the wealthy pay the majority of the taxes and make the majority of the donations to charities. Saying that they have been taking advantage of the rest of us is unfair. I heard yet another Democratic pundit on TV say that the rich should actually pay *more* than their fair share. I have to say, I'm concerned about the growing number of people who believe that the only way to be fair is to do *more* than what's fair. That's easy to say when it applies to someone else, but it makes absolutely no sense.

How We *Really* Elect Presidents

As I mentioned earlier, there was a period of dominance for the Republican Party from Lincoln's election up to the election of Franklin Delano Roosevelt. However, since FDR, we've elected twelve presidents — six Democrats and six Republicans. If you don't count those who ascended to the position through either assassination or resignation, the presidency changed parties with each change of president save for one, from Ronald Reagan to George HW Bush.

On the surface, it looks as if the country makes dramatic swings every eight years, changing the party it endorses. Perhaps after FDR's long presidency, we don't trust having one party in power for more than the two terms constitutionally allowed to one president, so following a presidency of eight years with a new president from the same party must seem as if too much control would be given to that party for too long a time.

Looking back at the presidential races in my lifetime, we see something more interesting. The losing candidates all had something in common. First, we should eliminate the incumbents who lost. They tend to lose based on how they are perceived or how people feel the country is doing. As Clinton famously said, "It's the economy, stupid."

So, let's remove the unsuccessful re-election campaigns of Ford, Carter, and George HW Bush from the discussion. For the remaining candidates, it may be more accurate to say that they lost the election rather than to say the president beat them. Looking closer, we find that many voters were voting against these candidates more than they were voting for the eventual winner. In other words, the president-elect had become the 'lesser' in the cliché, "The lesser of two evils."

This is not to say that the best man won in each case. What I'm saying is we have the benefit of time to look at what the winner did as president and decide whether they were good or not. At the time of the election people didn't have that luxury. So, armed only with what was known, the voters went to the polls. When reviewing the campaigns, it's no surprise that these candidates lost. Most made major campaign mistakes, had unpopular stances on issues, or were unpopular within their own party. Some went up against a president who was perceived as doing well and managing a successful economy or a president who was dealing with a major issue that changed the focus of the campaign.

As a rule, Independents can be swayed by many factors; however, the base usually stays loyal. In the case of many of these candidates, something happened that either caused them to lose most of the Independents, part of their base, or both. Let's take a look back.

In 1972, George McGovern challenged President Nixon. He seemed to have lost some of his support within the party after the 1968 Democratic National Convention in Chicago. While the primary is often a contentious race, his support diminished to the point that there was a group of Democrats campaigning as 'Democrats for Nixon'. McGovern also nominated Thomas Eagleton as his vice president. When it was revealed that Eagleton had suffered from clinical depression, McGovern vowed to stand by him, but with concern over the cold war and having him next in line, McGovern ditched him a few days later for Sargent Shriver. McGovern was also dealing with a strong economy and although running as an anti-war candidate, Nixon had already ended our involvement in the Vietnam War. Lastly, he accepted the Democrat nomination at three in the morning to virtually no viewers. With the loss of many moderate Democrats, McGovern never had a chance. Nixon won 49 states and 520 electoral votes.[124]

In 1984, it was Walter Mondale's turn to challenge a sitting Republican. Mondale was vice-president under Carter when Reagan won his first term, and now he was the challenger. He started with a historic VP pick, Geraldine Ferraro, who would have been the first female vice-president. The pick was expected to garner additional support for his campaign but was overshadowed by a controversy over her finances. He then ran a Liberal campaign when most candidates move to the center for the general election. In his acceptance speech at the Democratic National Convention, Mondale vowed to raise taxes, saying, "Mr. Reagan will raise taxes and so will I. He won't tell you. I just did." Many people didn't like talk of raising taxes and had no way to know that he was right about Reagan eventually raising taxes.

The Reagan campaign also was successful in convincing middle-class Americans that Mondale planned to fund programs for the poor at their expense. Most popularly, Mondale questioned Reagan's age and after performing well in the first debate, Reagan turned things permanently in the second debate. When asked by Henry Pruitt (*Baltimore Sun*), "Is there any doubt in your mind that you would be able to function in such circumstances," (Citing that Kennedy had to go days on end with very little sleep during the Cuban Missile Crisis, he also mentioned that Reagan was already the oldest president in history as well as the fact that Reagan's staff said he was tired after the first debate.) Reagan said, "Not at all, Mr. Pruitt, and I want you to know that also, I will not make age an issue of this campaign. I am not going to exploit, for political purposes, my opponent's youth and inexperience." The campaign ended with that statement. Reagan won 49 states and 525 electoral votes.[125]

In 1988, Michael Dukakis, Governor of Massachusetts, won the Democratic nomination. He was viewed as a weak governor and was a self-proclaimed "Proud Liberal". He was not prepared for the tough campaign Bush would run. President Bush portrayed Dukakis as not only a Liberal but as an elitist. Then, when Bush accused him of being weak on the military, Dukakis staged a photo in which he rode in an M1 Abrams tank. This move backfired and he was mocked for the so-called, "Snoopy Incident". Another blunder occurred when Dukakis' deputy field director Donna Brazile told reporters that President Bush needed to 'fess up' to the rumors of his extramarital affair. Dukakis fired Brazile, but this had dealt his campaign another blow.

The final dagger came when the Bush campaign ran a series of ads attacking Dukakis for commuting the sentences of murderers, many of whom re-offended. The Willie Horton ad was the most damaging and became the template for attack ads going forward. Following this, in the second debate, Bernard Shaw asked Dukakis, an opponent of capital punishment, if he would support the death penalty if his wife were raped and murdered. Dukakis didn't answer the question directly, but instead he talked about the ineffectiveness of capital punishment. Bush went on to win 40 states and 426 electoral votes.[126]

In 1996, Kansas Senator Bob Dole won the Republican nomination. This race was never really close, as the economy was going well and it was unlikely that voters were going to switch. Dole, like Mondale whose campaign was too Liberal, ran an extremely Conservative campaign, promising a 15% across-the-board reduction in income tax rates, and he drew criticism from both sides for his plan to include the Human Life Amendment, which would overturn Roe v. Wade. Clinton won 31 states and 379 electoral votes, and that's with a third party candidate, Ross Perot, getting over 8 million votes.[127]

In 2000, Al Gore won the Democratic nomination. He was the sitting vice-president serving under a popular president. How could he lose? He started with two small problems. The first was a personality problem. He had a reputation for being a stiff person who didn't mind telling you he was the smartest guy in the room. The second problem was the same as one of his strengths — Clinton. Although Clinton was very popular amongst Democrats, his recent impeachment over the sex-scandal caused Gore to distance himself from the President. Gore easily won the nomination, winning all of the primaries, and he selected Senator Joe Lieberman of Connecticut as his vice-presidential running mate. He tried to run a populist campaign and, unlike many candidates, had a detailed plan for how he wanted to govern. Much of what he wanted to do was very highbrow and did not get the attention of the American people. Once George Bush won the nomination, the two agreed on three debates. As would be expected, Gore was heavy on details while Bush came off as more genuine. Most thought Gore won the first debate and lost the second. In the third debate, Bush looked more in command while Gore seemed mean and aggressive.

The race remained close throughout, but the economic downturn in September followed by the USS Cole attack in October took some of the luster off the Clinton presidency, and Gore could not distance himself from it. The last hit came from Ralph Nader, Green Party candidate, getting 2.7% of the vote. Bush won 30 states and 272 electoral votes but lost the popular vote by over 500,000 votes.[128]

In 2004, John Kerry became the Democratic nominee and, after the bitter loss of 2000, was shouldering the burden of bringing the Democrats what was rightfully theirs. He ran a safe campaign of "I'm not George Bush" and never really had a platform. The Bush campaign tried to paint him as a flip-flopper for changing his position on Iraq. A group of veterans known as the 'Swift Boat Veterans for Truth' began running ads attacking Kerry for his allegations of war crimes during Vietnam and declaring him unfit to serve. They also challenged the legitimacy of his combat medals. In the aftermath of the 9/11 attacks, this deeply hurt his campaign.

At the same time, there were accusations that Bush did not fulfill his required service in the Air National Guard. This could have proved harmful to Bush but was negated by the larger story of CBS News using doctored documents in its *60 Minutes* story. The subsequent review led to the firing of the news producer and the resignation of notable anchor Dan Rather. Bush won 31 state and 286 electoral votes.[129]

In 2008, John McCain fought a tough primary to win the Republican nomination. He had been behind several times and was poorly funded but somehow beat the tough competition of Huckabee, Romney, and Giuliani. He had a hard time with the base of the party because he wasn't seen as Conservative enough. Much of this had to do with his stance on campaign finance reform and the Comprehensive Immigration Reform Act of 2007, which many Republicans equated to Amnesty.

Barak Obama was also in a hard-fought primary campaign, but once he was declared the victor, his party rallied around him. McCain, ever the underdog, was dogged by the hatred of the Bush presidency. So when President Bush endorsed him on March 5, 2008, that made it more difficult for him to maintain the label of an outsider. Running behind in the polls, McCain decided to go with a bold pick and chose Alaska Governor Sarah Palin as his running mate on August 29, 2008. This helped McCain with the Republican base and gave his campaign a bump for a brief moment, but once the media began to vet her, she didn't seem prepared and the excitement waned. In September of 2008, the financial crisis began and put additional blame on the Bush Administration, something from which McCain could not recover.

Race also played a part in the election, with Obama being the first non-White party nominee. An increased number of minorities and young voters participated in the election. There was no doubt that racists voted for the White candidate, but this was more than offset by the great number of people casting a vote for history. Obama won 28 states and 365 electoral votes.[130]

There's another interesting phenomenon at play in these elections. Most people feel an obligation to vote, but they really don't know the issues. So what is the best way to pick a president if you can't decide who would be the best person for the job? Vote for the guy you like the best. Take a closer look:

> Carter v. Reagan
> Clinton v. HW Bush & Dole
> Bush v. Gore & Kerry
> Obama v. McCain & Romney

Reagan was far more charismatic than Carter. Clinton had the same advantage over both Bush and Dole. He also made them look really old. Age was not a factor in the Bush v. Gore race, but Gore came off as an intellectual while Bush seemed like an average guy. Obama was the cool candidate. He made McCain look old, and Romney seemed cold and stiff in comparison. This is how we truly pick our candidates; being liked is more important than being right on the issues.

Being president is an unbelievably great responsibility, and how we judge them can sometimes be skewed. If he's not the guy you voted for, you complain about his policies, even if he did exactly what he said he would do when campaigning. If your candidate wins, you complain that he changed his course and didn't accomplish what he promised he would. In either case, the term of the presidency is an overwhelming mix of issues, events, and crises. Every president is faced with the task of delegating problems, making personnel decisions, and compromising to get things done. They also have to shift priorities based on the information of a given day — all of this while being the head of state in addition to the chief executive.

Each president may have handled a different aspect of the job better than others and will have his own unique place in U.S. history. Some will be viewed favorably but others poorly. Whatever your views on a particular president, it is only logical to assume that he took the office with the intent to guide the country in a positive direction. It's also difficult to compare them to each other since the conditions vary so much for each.

The bottom line is, each president will have his own set of successes and failures, but when the losing side is frustrated with the president, they tend to look back to the election and think, *What if?* The grass always looks greener on the other side, but history has proven that most often the voters are not overly excited by either candidate and tend to vote for the less distasteful of the two. It can be that the candidate is too Liberal, as were McGovern and Mondale, or too Conservative, as were Dole and Goldwater. It may just be that the candidate made too many mistakes in his campaign or the public didn't like him. But there has to be a reason why the public chose the guy who won, most of the time in an overwhelming fashion. We also tend to spend too much time looking at the negatives of a presidency instead of looking at it in its entirety. Such is the case with the next subject, George W. Bush.

George W. Bush

You may wonder why there is an entire chapter on George W. Bush. After all, the book is supposed to be about how Blacks and the Republicans need each other. Well, the common ground between the two is being blurred by the misconceptions toward Republicans, and who is a better example of all the misconceptions about Republicans?

Bush is wealthy. He's a racist (Kanye West told us he didn't care about Black people.). He spoke candidly and often about his faith, so he must be a religious zealot. He was against all of the social programs the Liberals fought to protect, and he got us into the longest war in our country's history. Bush is the walking embodiment of all the misconceptions about Republicans. And the icing on the cake is that he never should have been president in the first place, because — he stole the election.

George Walker Bush was the most hated man in America from 2000 until the early part of 2010. He received criticism from both sides of the aisle, while his policies were attacked, and he was blamed for every negative outcome the country faced from the end of 2000 to the present. He also endured the most vicious

161

personal attacks toward any president in recent history — maybe ever — but why?

Was he really as bad as his critics made him out to be? Do a Google search, and many results will list him as the worst president in history. When his presidency is taken as a whole, using logic and not emotion as the framework, it's hard to get there. There is no doubt that mistakes were made and that he had many detractors, but that is a trait of every presidency. But the hatred was deep-seated, angry, unapologetic, and absent of reality. Regardless of your views on Bush, can he really be worse than presidents who advanced slavery, caused the Great Depression, were overtly corrupt, or slaughtered innocent Native Americans to grow the country? And let's not forget those who died early in their presidencies. While there are many things that can be debated on both sides about Bush's presidency, most of the complaints came down to the following four points: the stolen election, the war, Hurricane Katrina, and the economy.

The stolen election

This came down to the fact that most people didn't understand the election process and the election results hinged on the one state, Florida, where Bush's brother was governor. Conspiracy theorists believed that Jeb Bush was able to guarantee the victory over Gore.

There has long been a debate about the Electoral College and whether it is an aide or a hindrance to the election process. Opponents say it negates the importance of the individual vote, gives too much credence to swing states, and discourages turnout. Proponents say it maintains balance from the larger cities, enhances the vote of minorities, and diminishes the effects of voter fraud. Both sides have valid points and the system could probably be tweaked a bit.

For instance, all but two states, Maine and Nebraska, are winner-takes-all states, meaning that if a candidate won the popular vote in California by only one vote, for example, he would win all 55 electoral votes. This may seem a bit unfair, but the same is true for using only the popular vote. If a candidate won the most populous cities, which is possible since most urban areas are Democratic, he would have a much easier path to win the election. This diminishes the value of voters in small states.

The congressional district method could be the best compromise, allowing the vote from each congressional district to go to the candidate who wins the popular vote in that district. The winner of the overall vote in the state would get the two additional electoral votes that represent the U.S. Senate seats. This would increase the belief that everyone's vote counts, which would improve turnout and limit the swing-state effect. It would also maintain the balance between large and small states while giving a better representation of the political voice of the country. Democrats would still lose Texas but would win several districts in Dallas, Houston, and Austin. Republicans would lose New York and California but get some electoral votes from upstate New York and Conservative areas of southern California. This makes virtually every state a swing state. Since this is not the case, we have to follow the process that is in place. This means a candidate can win the election without winning the popular vote. This had happened twice before, in 1876 and 1888.[131] So, like it or not, it's not as if the Republicans created a new law so that Bush could win.

As far as the conspiracy, it just seems too large of a cover-up to never have been leaked. Let's assume that Jeb Bush made a concerted effort to misplace, alter, or destroy ballots. He wouldn't have been able to do it himself, so he would have needed assistance in several polling places and several districts. This takes manpower and planning. I'm not naïve enough to think that it's out of the question to believe someone would try to rig an election. I just don't see how no one would have found out and reported it. Also, if we make the leap that Governor Bush was able to rig the ballots, he'd also have to do the same thing with the recount.

Finally, if we assume all of this is possible, then we'd have to guess that George Bush had no knowledge of what was happening. It would be a bit far-fetched to think that he asked his brother to cheat for him, and it would be as illogical for Jeb to tell him since the more layers you add to the deception the greater the chance that someone would find out.

Since there was no Bush conspiracy to steal votes in Florida, then why was there so much anger from it? People acted as if Gore won by a large margin and Bush was just appointed president in spite of this. Look at the facts: Gore did win the popular vote by just over 500,000 votes, but this is due to the largest cities in the country voting primarily Democrat. Bush won 30 states. That's not one or two states; that's a 10 state margin. Obama only won 28 states in 2008. Let's also remember that they had a do-over in 2004, and if the country was so upset that he had cheated in 2000, Bush should have lost by a large margin. Instead, in fact, he gained support. Whatever your thoughts on the presidential election of 2000, saying Bush stole the election is completely wrong.

The War

After the bitter election results, the divide between the parties was magnified. Because of the partisanship that became the norm going forward, everything the administration did that could be debated was scrutinized intensely. Anything that was considered universally positive was downplayed. This led to a one-sided view of Bush and a massive blame game that was about to get worse.

On September 11, 2001, the most devastating attack on U.S. soil occurred. The ramifications of those attacks on the psyche of the American people, on the course of government going forward, and on the country as a whole, cannot be expressed by words here due to both the brevity of this book and my lack of intellectual capacity to fully comprehend and explain all of the possible effects. One thing did seem certain: The attacks would bring the country together and divert the focus from all of the infighting and partisanship. Unfortunately, it turned out to be short-lived.

After the dust settled, blame came from every corner — all directed at President Bush. He was blamed for not reacting fast enough once informed of the attacks, the government retaliation and how that was handled, overreaching his executive powers, and even the attacks themselves. There were accusations of torture, the Abu Ghraib situation,[132] criticism of the Patriot Act,[133] and the popular vociferation when discussing weapons of mass destruction, "Bush lied; people died." While it's always good to question our leaders and challenge what is perceived as wrong, this must be done logically and evenly.

Whatever you think about the reaction to the attacks, blaming the fact that they happened on Bush seems like a stretch. Are we to believe that he was sworn in on January 20, 2001, Al Qaeda decided after that to attack us in the detailed and organized manner that they did, planned it, funded it, picked the date, and trained for it in just under eight months? As the commander-in-chief, Bush had to take responsibility for what happened on his watch, but I find it odd that no blame was placed at the feet of President Clinton, unless we believe that the intelligence agencies were concerned about an impending attack and were diligently searching for details but the new president told them it was no longer necessary to be concerned about terror attacks, but that is what some accused.

In his book, *Lies and the Lying Liars Who Tell Them*, then comedian and now Minnesota Senator Al Franken chronicled how President Clinton put a plan together to take out al Qaeda. Then, in the chapter titled "Operation Ignore", where he accuses the Bush Administration of ignoring all of the intelligence they were given, he said this, ". . . Berger (Clinton's National Security Advisor) arranged ten briefings for his successor, Condoleezza Rice, and her deputy, Stephen Hadley. Berger made a special point of attending the briefing on terrorism. He told Dr. Rice, 'I believe that the Bush Administration will spend more time on terrorism in general, and on al Qaeda specifically, than any other subject.' "[134]

In his ridicule of Bush, Franken actually helps the president's case. In the barrage of criticism he received, President Bush was mostly attacked for unnecessarily getting us into war and launching an unnecessary war on 'terrorism'. Sounds as if Senator Franken doesn't think Bush moved fast enough in going after terrorists. At one point he also suggested that Reagan didn't respond strongly enough to terror attacks during his presidency and that Bush Sr. should have gone into Afghanistan instead of allowing it to become a terrorist breeding ground. Wow, and I thought *Republicans* loved war.

On October 12, 2000, the USS *Cole* was bombed in a suicide attack, killing 17 and injuring 39.[135] The bombing was attributed to Bin Laden with help from the Sudanese Government. This reminds me that I need to self-edit something I said earlier when dispelling the misconception of Republicans and war. I said that we *always* retaliate when we are attacked. This is one of the few times we did not. Much has been written about this in the years since, and it's been documented that Clinton, in the days after the attack, was advised to strike back and decided against it.

Clinton decided to methodically attack the whole organization rather than simply retaliating as usual. Many say this bombing of the *Cole* was a direct cause of the 9/11 attacks, either because Bin Laden was emboldened by its success or bothered by the lack of retaliation and felt it wasn't taken seriously enough. Months later, when Bush took office, he also decided against the advice. National Security Advisor Condoleezza Rice told the 9/11 Commission, "All that I can tell you is that what the president wanted was a plan to eliminate al Qaeda, so he could stop swatting at flies. He knew that we had in place the same crisis management mechanism indeed, the same personnel that the Clinton administration, which clearly thought it a very high priority, had in place. And so I think that he saw the priority as continuing the current operations and then getting a plan in place."[136] It doesn't sound as if Bush ignored the threats or asked the intelligence community to stop what Clinton had started. Either way, it seems impossible to pin this solely on Bush.

167

One conspiracy that I must admit is not a great leap is that of Bush wanting to invade Iraq for personal reasons. I don't believe it, but I see how people can get there. Saddam Hussein did try to kill his father and was an all-around nasty guy. The implication that Bush lied about the weapons of mass destruction to coerce Congress and the country to go to war with Iraq is most likely incorrect, but at least highly inflated. He may have interpreted the intelligence incorrectly or tried to unfairly link Iraq to the 9/11 attacks, but to think he blatantly lied about Iraq having weapons with the sole purpose of coercing Congress to go to war, we'd have to discount a very relevant government official who felt the same way, President Clinton.

Clinton signed the Iraq Liberation Act, which had a goal of removing the current regime and supporting democracy in Iraq. In a speech to the Joint Chiefs of Staff, President Clinton said this:

"Iraq repeatedly made false declarations about the weapons that it had left in its possession after the Gulf War. When UNSCOM would then uncover evidence that gave lie to those declarations, Iraq would simply amend the reports. For example, Iraq revised its nuclear declarations four times within just 14 months and it has submitted six different biological warfare declarations, each of which has been rejected by UNSCOM. In 1995, Hussein Kamal, Saddam's son-in-law, and the chief organizer of Iraq's weapons of mass destruction program, defected to Jordan. He revealed that Iraq was continuing to conceal weapons and missiles and the capacity to build many more. Then and only then did Iraq admit to developing numbers of weapons in significant quantities and weapon stocks. Previously, it had vehemently denied the very thing it just simply admitted once Saddam Hussein's son-in-law defected to Jordan and told the truth. Now listen to this, what did it admit? It admitted, among other things, an offensive biological warfare capability notably 5,000 gallons of botulinum, which causes botulism; 2,000 gallons of anthrax; 25 biological-filled Scud warheads; and 157 aerial bombs. And I might say UNSCOM inspectors believe that Iraq has actually greatly understated its production. As if we needed further confirmation, you all know what happened to his son-in-law when he made the untimely decision to go back to Iraq. Next, throughout this entire process, Iraqi agents have undermined and undercut UNSCOM. They've harassed the inspectors, lied to them, and disabled monitoring cameras, literally spirited evidence out of the back doors of suspect facilities as inspectors walked through the front door. And our people were there observing it and had the pictures to prove it. Despite Iraq's deceptions, UNSCOM has nevertheless done a remarkable job. Its inspectors the eyes and ears of the civilized world have uncovered and destroyed more weapons of mass destruction capacity than was destroyed during the Gulf War. This includes nearly 40,000 chemical weapons, more than 100,000 gallons of chemical weapons agents, 48 operational missiles, 30 warheads specifically fitted for chemical and biological weapons, and a massive biological weapons facility at Al Hakam equipped to produce anthrax and other deadly agents."[137]

This is not to say that Clinton was in full support of the war, since he even warned of the dangers, but it only points to the claims the critics made. They weren't attacking Bush about going to war; they were claiming that he lied about the weapons. As far as the war itself; it's not as if he just unilaterally attacked Iraq. The resolution was passed by a majority vote in Congress.[138] So if we went to war based on a lie, it was also Congress and not just Bush who lied.

People also criticized the way the war was being handled. They questioned whether we should be in Iraq, if we used enough troops, where the focus should be, etc. I was amazed to see so many Americans, many of whom could not even name the senators from their state, had become authorities on foreign policy overnight. The chants of "Bush lied; people died" intensified, and the high approval ratings he had after the attacks started to decline. He was feeling the heat from everywhere, and it was about to get worse.

Hurricane Katrina

After his 2004 win, which many attributed to Republicans scaring people into believing that Kerry wouldn't keep them safe, things started to normalize a bit. Though he was still being attacked, much of it personal, the level of animus had decreased. Then the storm of the century hit.

In August of 2005, Hurricane Katrina developed in the Atlantic. It made landfall in Florida as a category 1 hurricane but briefly strengthened to a category 5 storm over the Gulf. On August 29th, Katrina again made landfall as a category 3 hurricane, devastating areas from Florida to Texas with most of its impact being felt in Louisiana and Mississippi. When the storm hit New Orleans, the levees were breached causing 80% of the city to flood. The rescue was slow, and the resulting tragedy led to 1833 deaths and nearly $80 billion in damages.[139]

While the criticism of the response was warranted and the loss of life was devastating, it seemed that all of the blame was directed at President Bush. While the federal government should have done a better job, and the president rightfully gets the blame for their performance, we view this with the knowledge of hindsight. When you consider the information as it was becoming available and the facts of the response, it becomes more difficult to adequately place blame.

The level of destruction that a natural disaster will cause cannot be predicted. It is therefore best to be prepared for the worst-case scenario. The preparation for Katrina was not enough. On August 26, the National Hurricane Center projected that Katrina's path was the Florida Panhandle. The following day, the plan was revised to Southeast Louisiana. This could have caused a slight delay in the government's response, as the National Response Plan dictates that disaster planning and response is the responsibility of the local government.

Once warned of the severity of the storm, Mayor Ray Nagin declared a state of emergency and called for a voluntary evacuation. The day before the storm hit, he issued the city's first-ever whole-city mandatory evacuation order. Although he was criticized for not issuing the evacuation order soon enough, the real issue was the combination of a lack of planning to get those out who needed assistance and the refusal of some to leave.[140] For areas such as New Orleans that have to deal with hurricanes on an annual basis, residents often feel that they can ride the storm out. As for those who needed help, the mayor issued a mandatory evacuation decree that couldn't be carried out.

Louisiana Governor Kathleen Blanco garnered some blame for not declaring a state of emergency soon enough or allowing the federal government to nationalize the Louisiana National Guard.[141] Some of this blame was warranted — some not. While the president did declare a state of emergency on August 27th, the federal government did not seem to do enough or act swiftly enough to minimize the loss of life. What turned out to be worse for him than the actual events of the recovery were his actions in the wake of the storm. The president continued with his vacation and scheduled events on Medicare and Iraq instead of returning to Washington D.C. as some thought he should.[142] This gave the perception that he lacked leadership.

The only way to guarantee the safety of the residents of New Orleans was to evacuate them; however, there is no realistic way to evacuate tens of thousands of people in less than 24 hours. The national response was also transferred to the Department of Homeland Security, an agency that had only been in existence for two years. There is a bigger issue here; the government never really tries to prepare for a crisis. They simply put something in place afterwards in hopes of preventing a similar crisis from happening again, yet we continue to put our hopes in the government to quickly respond when we need them.

President Bush should have done a better job in his reaction to Katrina, as should have the local and state levels of government; however, it is unfair to say that the slow reaction was based on race. The storm hit an area with over 15 million residents, so it did not only affect Blacks. As for New Orleans, people are underestimating how fast the water that breached the levees would fill an area that is already below sea level. Many of those who died were Black because they happened to be the residents of that area, and not because the president didn't care about them.

The Economy

When Bush took office in 2001 there was a surplus, and when he left in 2009 there was a deficit. However, when the economy tanked in late 2007 and the housing bubble burst, everything was blamed on Bush. People said that the economic slide was due to the Bush policies that eased regulations and allowed this to happen. As was typical for the Bush critics, they had no use for facts in these claims.

First, there was the dot-com bubble. In the 1990s, there was a craze over the Internet's growing popularity, and many investors gave money to Internet start-ups who claimed to have creative ways to market and sell products on the Internet. This created a rush for the newest Internet gimmicks, and with it, the dot-com boom. Some start-ups failed quickly and never got off the ground, while others took of immediately. Many of those companies that were successful, however, spent too much time advertising and trying to gain users instead of focusing on a revenue stream. By January 2000 the bubble had burst, and many of the Internet companies had gone out of business, resulting in millions of dollars in losses. Some of these companies were: Webvan, Kozmo.com, and pets.com.[143]

If the rise and fall of the dot-coms wasn't enough, there were the companies who just flat out defrauded their way to billions in profits. The well-known Enron, WorldCom, and subsequent

Arthur Andersen scandals are remembered as part of Bush's Presidency, but we all forget that the illegal activities for which these companies were found guilty happened long before Bush was president. The collapse and trials were the only parts that took place during his presidency.

The combination of the dot-com burst and the financial corruption that was uncovered took a toll on the market. From September 2000 to January 2001, while Clinton was still president, the NASDAQ lost over 45% of its value, and by October 2002, an estimated 8 trillion dollars in wealth was lost. Whenever the government seems to have made a mistake, allowing someone to get hurt, they over-regulated to compensate for it. In this case, the "mistake" was made by President Clinton and the "over-regulation" was implemented by President Bush.

As a result of the corporate scandals of Enron, Adelphia, and WorldCom, President Bush signed the Sarbanes-Oxley Act in 2002 to increase oversight on corporate governance. In October of 2008, another financial collapse was underway. This crash was due primarily to a mortgage crisis. While much of this was again blamed on Bush, the only legislations he passed that were financial in nature were the American Dream Down Payment Act, the Bankruptcy Reform Act, and the Pension Protection Act. None of these had anything to do with bank regulations or how they lent money.

The legislation that was most closely connected to the mortgage crisis had been signed by President Clinton. The Gramm Leach Bliley Act and the Commodity Futures Modernization Act of 2000 repealed part of the Glass-Steagall Act of 1933 and deregulated the financial services industry, which critics, including President

Obama, believe all led to the subprime mortgage issues and created companies that were later deemed too big to fail.[144]

Even if we assume that Bush softened legislation against Wall Street, is it logical to assume that only Republicans voted to pass these new regulations or that only Republican bankers and hedge fund managers took advantage of them? These problems were too big to be caused by one person, and while Bush's level of blame for all of the crises of his presidency can be debated, it is obvious that the only reason Bush gets all of the blame for these events is that Liberals decided that they hated him, and they tend to base their opinions on emotion rather than fact. How else can you explain how a detailed look into the events that happened in the course of the Bush presidency led everyone to blame the Bush administration alone? Some things started under Clinton. Congress had to vote on legislation, and sometimes people have to take part of the blame, as should those who bought more house than they could afford or those who refused to evacuate New Orleans when warned.

As did many people, I had criticisms of Bush during his presidency. My biggest issue was not anything the Liberals or Conservatives were pointing out. It was on a grander scale. I didn't think there was an overriding theme to his presidency. Most prior presidents had some issue or greater movement they wanted to focus on during their term. Polk and Benjamin Harrison had expanding the country in mind, while FDR had the New Deal. Lyndon Johnson had the Great Society, and Reagan's focus was ending the Cold War. What was Bush's theme? I realized however, that his presidency never really got off the ground before events occurred that would have diverted focus away from his plans anyway.

I gained respect for President Bush after his presidency, because through all of the tough times and situations that challenged his resolve, he never blamed anyone else and often shouldered the blame when it wasn't his. Also, when people made vicious, personal attacks on him, he never showed any animosity or consternation, and, in light of it all, he was able to make fun of himself. This turned out to be a much needed trait, for as much as everyone from both parties talked about respecting the office of the presidency, their actions left me scratching my head.

Respecting the Office of the Presidency

From a performance standpoint, I think the same thing about Obama as I did about Bush. I think the opposite party, in this case the Republicans, often go too far in criticizing the president. But no one can honestly say he is doing a bang-up job. Most Liberal Democrats would say that he either didn't do enough of the things they expected from him, that he didn't go far enough on the ones he did pursue, or that he did nothing when he should have taken action. These are the same things Conservatives in the Republican Party said about Bush.

There was something strangely different, however, in the way they were scrutinized. The Republicans attacked President Obama from the onset. Though many of the attacks were unfair, consisting of that popular lie by omission that was addressed earlier, most were directed toward his policies and performance. Even when some pundit stooped to ad hominem attacks, those attacks were more in the form of, "He's a Socialist," or, "He wants to take the country in the wrong direction," rather than the debasing comments we heard about Bush.

As for the Democrats, they almost completely abstained from questioning the president's actions, and when things happened that were eerily similar to situations during Bush's presidency, both positive and negative, the response was dramatically different. Not only was the response from the Democrats different, but the media coverage was also different. Much of the change in how politics is viewed started with a shift in the news coverage.

In the 1980s, CNN was launched as the first 24-hour news network. 24-hour coverage allowed for many more stories and the advent of specific shows that covered a range of topics. *Crossfire* was one of these shows. *Crossfire* enlisted two political pundits, one from the Left and one from the Right, to discuss issues of the day. Much of this would consist of short arguments on both sides.

In 1996, right in the middle of the Clinton Presidency, the Fox News Channel was introduced. It was started by Rupert Murdoch and Roger Ailes as an alternative to the mainstream news shows and CNN, a network they believed was biased to the Left. Fox changed news reporting by going completely away from the anchor desk format and bringing in guests for each topic, often from both sides to heed their slogan of 'Fair and Balanced'.

CNN was now in a ratings war and would slowly adapt the same format to compete. The combination of the ratings battle, the growth of reality 'shock' TV, and the popularity of the Internet forever changed how we got the news.

In the early 2000s, talk radio started to grow, with many Conservative hosts following in Rush Limbaugh's footsteps. In 2004, Air America was created as a Liberal alternative, and though it dissolved in 2010, many Progressive shows remained. Now the stage was set for a nonstop influx of information. Unfortunately, much of it was incomplete and partisan, and few people took time to vet what they were hearing.

We often hear that people should respect the office of the presidency. What we're never told is that there is a caveat: It only counts when *your* guy is in office. During Clinton's second term, he received what I thought at the time to be the most egregious attacks on a sitting president. Republican pundits on news stations and much of talk radio attacked his character, called him a liar, and said he was an embarrassment to the country. When talking about him, many called him "Slick Willy" instead of identifying him as the president, and they started a call to have him impeached. Democrats responded simply by saying that it was just an affair, so even though it was wrong, the Republicans are making too much of it and that Clinton was still a good president.

Then, Bush became president and I was proven wrong; apparently the attacks could get worse. It started with him being a cheater, not only for stealing the election but for skirting his duties in the Texas National Guard and for his time in college where he only got in because of his dad. The attacks grew to him being a liar due to the war, an idiot due to his frequent misstatements, and even a racist.

While this seemed a bit extreme, it was only a little worse than what Clinton endured. What made the attacks on Bush different is that celebrities started to believe that it was their duty to speak out about politics and didn't feel they needed to respect the office of the presidency.

Dixie Chicks singer, Natalie Maines, said she was ashamed the president was from Texas, and after making an apology, she retracted it in 2006 saying, ". . . I don't feel that way anymore. I don't feel he is owed any respect whatsoever . . ." Commenting on Natalie Maines, Linda Ronstadt said, "The Dixie Chicks said they were embarrassed he was from Texas. I'm embarrassed George Bush is from the United States."

In September of 2006, Venezuelan President Hugo Chavez, when speaking to the UN General Assembly, said this about President Bush, "The Devil came here yesterday, and it smells of sulfur still today." While that may be considered disrespectful to say on the international stage, what's more telling is the visits Chavez has received from Kevin Spacey, Sean Penn, Danny Glover, Harry Belafonte, and Cornell West.

I can go on and on with the list of comments and attacks, but the point has been made. And I'm not arguing against their right to say what they want in a free society. I just want people to admit that there is a double standard. Since President Obama was elected, he has had a lot of attacks from the Right. Some have been fair; some have gone too far, and some have been downright disrespectful. There is no way, however, that anyone can say that the attacks on Obama have been any worse than those on Clinton and definitely not worse than those on Bush — or can they?

In the beginning of Obama's first term, I got an odd feeling that people were tempering their comments so they wouldn't come off as racists. Republicans danced around some of their typical talking points, and even comedians were hesitant to poke fun at President Obama. Eventually, comedians found a way to make fun of Obama, usually by exaggerating the positive views that people have about him. And when the 2012 elections came around, the Republicans took the gloves off. Once this happened,

I immediately heard Blacks say things such as, "You've never seen a president disrespected like this president has been."

Hearing this shocked and slightly offended me. This was another example of Blacks going from demanding to be treated as equals to demanding to be treated better. After over a decade of rhetoric from both sides, is it now impossible to criticize the president without being a racist?

When Cornell West and Tavis Smiley challenged some of the decisions of the Obama Administration, they were criticized. This was in spite of Smiley's supporting the president and consistently saying his job is to "respect, protect, and correct" this president. I don't necessarily agree with the protect part. I have to give Smiley credit for at least leaving the door open to criticize Obama, but I feel that Smiley's mantra is wrong. It's important to respect and correct every president, and there's no reason to protect this president. The implication is that we as Blacks need to protect Obama from attacks, primarily racists ones. The most powerful man in the world does not need our protection. We should let the criticism come as it has with others, and when the criticism is over the top, simply disagree as you would any other unwarranted attack. I also disagree with the "This president . . ." statements that imply that whoever is in the office is not everyone's president.

What I find is that most Democrats either have their views and don't care what happens or they are hypocrites, and when the Democrats and Republicans do the same thing, they're okay with attacking the Republicans and saying nothing about the Democrats.

This, unfortunately, goes for voters on both sides. We pay more attention to what politicians say or what we hear about them then what they actually do. The odd thing is that this tends to help the Democrats and hurt the Republicans. As I stated when mentioning the misconceptions, people already believe that the Democrats are out to help minorities and the poor, and that the Republicans want to control social issues. Here are some interesting facts to consider.

Many Liberals disagreed with the Iraq war and hated Bush for getting us into it, again placing no blame on Congress who voted for it. However, Obama announced that he was ordering an additional 30,000 troops to Afghanistan, and routinely conducted Drone attacks in the Middle East, yet we've heard very little from the anti-war resistance.

When discussing the items he didn't get passed, they blamed the Republicans for blocking him even when the Democrats had a majority and the Republicans didn't have enough votes stop anything until 2010. In 2011 and 2012, Obama submitted budget proposals that didn't receive a single vote. Let me say that again: President Obama submitted two budget proposals, and not one person, Democrat or Republican, voted for them.

Then there's the auto bailout. There has been a debate about whether the auto bailout worked or not, but those who did agree with it praised Obama for it — when it was actually done by Bush. Since the Bush bailout was proposed in December of 2008, it had to be completed during Obama's term. You can give Obama some credit, but you cannot fairly exclude Bush. Liberals also hated Bush's PATRIOT ACT and the Bush Tax cuts, yet Obama extended them both, and still no complaints.

Speaking of the economic slide; much of how the market reacts is due to investor confidence. It is not always what you do but what you say. It is fair to argue that Bush's reaction to the financial meltdown caused unemployment to rise. The year ended at 7.2%. However, when Obama spoke about the economy and unemployment grew to 10%, he was able to also blame that on Bush. It can't be both ways; either you have to admit Bush did some good, or you have to admit that Obama's reaction had a detrimental effect.

This hypocrisy didn't start when Obama became president. During the Bush Presidency, he was described as a typical Right-wing zealot trying to control social issues. While president, the only legislation he signed involving social issues was the Partial Birth Abortion Ban Act limiting late-term abortions. While many Liberals may disagree with this act, it is hardly an evil plan to control women and overturn Roe v. Wade. However, it's interesting to note that Clinton signed much legislation that you would typically attribute to Republicans.

He signed the Violent Crime Control and Law Enforcement Act which created dozens of new offenses eligible for the death penalty and overturned a section of the Higher Education Act of 1965 permitting prison inmates to receive a Pell Grant for post-secondary education while incarcerated.

He also signed the Antiterrorism and Effective Death Penalty Act of 1996, which made it easier to apply the death penalty in certain cases, the Personal Responsibility and Work Opportunity Reconciliation Act, also called welfare reform, which added the work component to welfare, and the Defense of Marriage Act which defined marriage as between a man and a woman.

Lastly, the Democrats have done a great job of painting the Republicans as the fringe group who want to deport all of the

183

illegals, but little is said about the fact that Obama is on track to deport more illegals in his first term than Bush deported in both of his.

I don't point this out to say that either party is wrong or right. What is clear is that many voters, and most Black voters, are not using logic when forming their opinions. While it's easy to understand why people have an emotional response to things, it is not the most sensible course to take, and it limits the effectiveness of the government and those you elect to represent you.

Part IV

LOGIC,
SO WHAT NOW?

How Emotions Skew Our Opinions

There are definite divides on issues between the parties; however, the biggest difference is how they base their ideas. Liberals are emotion-based, while Conservatives are logic-based. Emotions are strong and can have a pronounced effect on your actions.

My wife and I were in the car just before the election, and I turned on a Black talk radio station. The show was being hosted by a former alderperson, and she was taking calls about the issues that affect the Black community. No less than three callers in a row made arguments against issues supported by President Obama.

The first expressed his disapproval of the Dream Act, the second her disgust with gay marriage, and the third her disdain with abortion rights, yet they all ended their calls with, "Vote for Obama." While this didn't surprise me, my wife was shocked. I listen to a lot of talk radio but she doesn't, so she hadn't heard this spelled out so clearly before. I told her this was common but that sometimes it gets worse.

On another occasion, I was listening to the *Matt McGill Show* on the same station, and he was discussing political issues in the Black community. A Black caller stated that he was upset with the job that congressman Jesse Jackson, Jr. was doing and would not be voting for him in the upcoming election. The host asked the caller who he was going to vote for, and the caller said, "The White woman who's running. I can't remember her name." At this point, Matt got really upset. He muted the caller and went on a tirade. He said, "What kind of Black person are you? See, this is one of our problems; we got boot licking niggers like you willing to vote for the White candidate over a Black candidate. Do you think having one less Black person in Congress will help the Black cause?" He went to commercial and never let the caller speak again. Jackson went on to win the election only to resign weeks later due to scandal.

Blacks are often told that voting Republican is voting against their best interest. This oversimplification assumes that we all have the same interests. No one expects all women to think the same or all Whites to think the same, but in the Black community, it's almost mandatory to vote Democrat. I have a few friends who agree with most of the Democratic platform, and while I disagree with them, I can respect them. They know what they believe and vote accordingly. But for most people, their votes have very little to do with their beliefs. Here's a conversation I had with someone very close to me.

Me: What are you doing?

X: Watching my man Obama!

Me: I guess you've decided who you're going to vote for?

X: Of course!

Me: Why?

X: Because he's smart and cool.

Me: That's not a reason to vote for someone. You don't think Romney's smart?

X: Well...

Me: You can't say *anything* positive about Romney?

X: No.

Me: Why, what's wrong with him?

X: He's a racist.

Me: What has he done that is racist?

X: It's not anything he's done; it's in the window.

Me: Excuse me?

X: You know; it's in his eyes, and I can read between the lines.

Me: You mean innuendo?

X: Yes.

How can you combat that? It defies logic. Republicans can have all the facts on their side, but it won't matter. People have to be open to hear the facts and consider other points of view, but people who think like this are not. If people can't overlook their prejudices and continue to judge others based solely on their biases, they will remain susceptible to bad information. Though this hurts the Republicans, the people who will suffer most are those who disregard the facts due to the strength of their emotions. This allows them to be guided blindly, and that is potentially dangerous for everyone.

This emotional approach causes most Blacks to unilaterally believe the Democrats and distrust the Republicans. Believing either party entirely doesn't make sense. In this election year, there was no shortage of political talk. It came up at dinner parties, at work, with friends — you couldn't escape it. I also listen to a lot of talk radio, Conservative and Progressive, so I heard many opinions. Very few of these opinions were based on facts.

I live in Chicago, so most of my circle is made up of Democrats. No one talked about the good job President Obama was doing. I either heard bad things about Romney and the Republicans or just the generic, "Obama has to win." 2008 was a historic election and the euphoria for Obama was understandable. Many Conservatives voted for Obama. What is odd is that very few people on the Left even question the Obama Administration. I, of course, find fault with the Obama presidency as I did with Bush. It's inevitable since no presidency is perfect. My concern is that emotion prevented millions of people from voting based on issues or logic.

Emotion causes people to generalize. When the Koch brothers wrote a letter to their employees stating that if Obama wins they may have to downsize, people were outraged. When Republican Senators Todd Akin and Richard Mourdock made outrageous comments about rape when discussing abortion, they were rightfully attacked. The problem in these cases is that people immediately generalized by saying that the beliefs of Akin, Mourdock, and the Koch brothers were reflective of the entire Republican Party. This is no different than a fellow Democrat saying something you don't believe and linking you to their comments. It is unfair and illogical to believe that these people speak for the majority of the Republican Party.

Emotion-based reasoning is also why most Blacks believe the misconceptions about Republicans. Why else would they constantly say that old White men are racists but only label the

190

Republican ones that way? How is it that Sheldon Adelson and Mitt Romney are racist but George Soros and John Kerry are not? The facts don't support these misconceptions, and having Republicans respond to accusations simply by saying that they aren't true won't change anyone's mind.

I had someone tell me they were voting for Democrats because they agree with Obama's plan to raise taxes on the rich. This is not uncommon. What surprised me is that this person believed that the rich paid no taxes. And after much lobbying on my part, they conceded that they probably pay some but would not believe that they pay more, both in gross amount and percentage, than the average American. While the debate rages between Democrats and Republicans as to how high the tax rate should be, at what income levels the rate should adjust, and what loopholes should be allowed, there is a segment of the population who believe the rich pay no taxes at all. How do you combat emotion when it's not accompanied by any facts?

Another way emotion skews our opinions is that it allows us to create double standards. When Limbaugh suggested in a debate over contraception that if Sandra Fluke was having so much sex that she couldn't afford her birth control then she must be a slut, advertisers left and there were calls to end his program. However, when Bill Maher called Sarah Palin a "Dumb twat" or when *Hustler* magazine showed a picture depicting Republican commentator S. E. Cupp engaged in a sex act with what appears to be a penis in her mouth, there was no call to cancel Maher's show and no one requested that newsstands remove Hustler magazine.

When Arizona Governor Jan Brewer put her finger in Obama's face, people were outraged, yet when an Iraqi reporter threw his shoes at President Bush, they laughed, and when Hugo Chavez called Bush the Devil — no outcry. In fact, we still have celebrities visiting Chavez in Venezuela. Where was Tavis Smiley's protection when Bush needed it?

When John Kerry won the Democratic nomination in 2004, we didn't hear an outcry to determine where he invested his money, yet they all clamored to find out where Romney's money, a much smaller sum, was invested.

Then there's the topic of Bush and Obama's education. Bush went to Yale for undergrad and then Harvard Business School, becoming the first and only president with an MBA. Many people contend that he was only accepted because of his father's clout. This is not totally implausible, but they look at his father as a former president, vice-president, and director of the CIA. Keep in mind that when George went away to college, his father was only one year into his first term in the House. When he was accepted at Harvard, his father was the Chairman of the Republican National Committee. That's not quite the power source people were thinking. I can't see people saying that Michael Steele or Reince Priebus had enough clout to get their kids accepted to Harvard without merit, but I'll leave the possibility open.

As for Obama, he went to Columbia and then Harvard Law School. Some people contend that he was an Affirmative Action student, an assertion that many of Obama's proponents find offensive. What's odd is that it seemed okay to imply that Harvard not only accepted Bush because of his family but somehow passed him through even though he was an idiot, but it's not okay to imply that Obama got into Harvard due to Affirmative Action programs, programs with which most of his supporters agree. How can you

192

be for Affirmative Action but still be ashamed of it? In any event, it seems as if their double standard was alive.

Lastly, emotion causes people to focus on what feels good rather than what's logical. They want a compassionate politician who will create a utopia. They care about others and want to help, but they are not focused on how this utopia will be created or whether the politicians they support are actually as compassionate as they think. Therefore, saying you care about Latinos works, especially if you use a Spanish accent, because it feels good even if your policies don't support it. It also works if you say you care about the poor, even if your policies don't support your comments. Once it was decided that the Democrats were the compassionate ones, it was assumed that anyone who agreed with the Republicans lacked empathy.

I often laugh when I hear a Liberal describe Conservatives as close-minded, crazy extremists who feel that everyone must conform to their way of thinking. I laugh because I hear it so often and because it better describes the Liberal mindset. It's obvious that I agree with some of the Republican platform, but not all. However, when I tell someone that I agree with some of the Republican views, they hear, "I agree with the Republicans," therefore I am evil.

Most Conservatives reach their views through logic, and while they are confident that they are right, they are open to the fact that they might be wrong. Liberals tend not to have that level of self-awareness. They are armed with compassion and see no reason to compromise. Some of them won't date a Republican, won't be friends with a Republican, and they judge them based on party affiliation alone. They boycott businesses that don't share their political views, and if someone they know and like admits to being a Republican, they ostracize them.

Then there are the attacks. Look at Stacy Dash: She came out in support of Mitt Romney and received vile attacks, such as, "Kill yourself," and, "You're an unemployed Black woman endorsing Mitt Romney. You're voting against yourself thrice, you poor, beautiful idiot."[145] How is it that the presidential candidate chosen by someone you don't even know can make someone this angry? It's because Liberals believe they are morally right and this gives them the right to force their opinions on others. In this case, the opinion is that if you're Black you must be a Democrat.

Whatever your views about Republicans, at least they play nicer when removed from politics. When was the last time you heard of a Republican refusing to see a movie because a Liberal was in it (unless it was Sean Penn)? It doesn't happen unless the person simply doesn't like that actor but not simply because he or she is a Democrat. Republicans listen to all kinds of music, but in politics, they are consigned to songs that are so old they no longer have proprietary obligations to them since none of the cool kids want Republicans playing their records. Springsteen, Petty, Sting, Rage Against the Machine, and Van Halen are just a few of the long list of recording artists who refused to let Republicans play their songs on the campaign trail. Really, don't be so petty, Tom.

Let's look at this year's debates. It can be argued that three of the four debates were moderated by Liberals. Even after Conservative talk show hosts pointed this out and questioned it, the Romney campaign agreed to participate in them. Imagine the uproar we would have heard if the debates had announced their moderators as Bill O'Reilly, Sean Hannity, and Amy Holmes.

194

At the end of the day, Conservatives are brought to their views through their values and logic. They are not afraid that being around Democrats will rub off on them. The Democrats, being feelings-based, are more likely to let their emotions guide them. This has also swept in a strange new political phenomenon — celebrity campaigning. Celebrities have always endorsed candidates but not with the volume and force of today. With the advent of reality TV and social media, people care what celebrities think, and celebrities overwhelmingly endorsed Obama. How did all of these celebrities become so knowledgeable about the issues, and, if we live in such a divided country, how is it that they are overwhelmingly one-sided?

While all of the stars of stage, film, and music come out to endorse the Democrats, not only do we not hear complaints from the Republicans, but no one tells them to kill themselves. As for the Liberals, they just follow the celebrities' suggestions to the ballot box. And since none of the celebrities have time to do research for themselves, Liberals are left gambling on the fact that the good looks of Clooney, the cool factor of Jay-Z, and the collective wealth of Hollywood will be there to help them when they are wrong.

Why Blacks Need
the Republicans

"It is unfortunate, too, that such a large number of Negroes do not know any better than to stake their whole fortune on politics. History does not show that any race, especially a minority group, has ever solved an important problem by relying altogether on one thing, certainly not by parking its political strength on one side of the fence because of empty promises."[146] This statement from Dr. Carter G. Woodson's book, *Mis-Education of the Negro,* is as true now as it was when it was published in 1933.

The fact that Blacks vote monolithically for the Democratic Party has more to do with fear and misinformation than it does ideology. It can be argued that the majority of Blacks' views on issues are more in line with the Republicans than with the Democrats. While that statement can be debated, what cannot be debated is the fact that 95% of the Black community voting for Democrats is not indicative of the percentage of Blacks whose views align with the Democratic Party.

So why do Blacks do it? There's no way you can get any group together and get 95% of them to agree upon anything. So, logically, we know they aren't voting based on their beliefs. If we assume Blacks are split on the issues 60/40 between the views of Democrats and Republicans, why would 35%, those Blacks who don't agree with the Democratic policy, vote Democratic anyway?

It's the powerful and effective campaign of fear and misinformation the Democrats have exacted over the years. Fear is the most important component here, as without it, few would believe the misinformation. The fear was instilled by making Blacks believe that Republicans are racists, knowing that, based on our history, there's nothing we would despise more than a racist. Once Blacks were convinced that Republicans were deliberately trying to harm them, any amount of misinformation seemed feasible. While I don't believe that the accusations of racism are true, there are several reasons why some Blacks need to join the Republican Party in spite of the supposed racism.

First, logic tells us that just because a person is racist doesn't mean he or she is wrong. If a world-renowned chef, who's known to be a racist, gave you a recipe to perfect a difficult dish, would you discount his expertise based on the fact that he is a racist? One doesn't necessarily have anything to do with the other. I know this may be too simplistic, so here's a better example.

Abraham Lincoln has been credited for freeing the slaves. Because of this, he is praised in the Black community. He is considered a hero by many and for years has remained among the top of everybody's list of greatest presidents. However, no man is perfect, and in the fourth debate with Stephen Douglas, Lincoln said this:

198

"While I was at the hotel to-day, an elderly gentleman called upon me to know whether I was really in favor of producing a perfect equality between the Negroes and white people. [Great Laughter.] While I had not proposed to myself on this occasion to say much on that subject, yet as the question was asked me I thought I would occupy perhaps five minutes in saying something in regard to it."

I will say then that I am not, nor ever have been in favor of bringing about in anyway the social and political equality of the White and Black races — that I am not nor ever have been in favor of making voters or jurors of negroes, nor of qualifying them to hold office, nor to intermarry with White people; and I will say in addition to this that there is a physical difference between the White and Black races which I believe will forever forbid the two races living together on terms of social and political equality. And inasmuch as they cannot so live, while they do remain together there must be the position of superior and inferior and I, as much as any other man, am in favor of having the superior position assigned to the White race. I say upon this occasion I do not perceive that because the White man is to have the superior position the Negro should be denied everything."[147]

And in a letter to Horace Greeley, editor of the *New York Tribune*, replying to an editorial he had written, Lincoln wrote:

"I would save the Union. I would save it the shortest way under the Constitution. The sooner the national authority can be restored; the nearer the Union will be "the Union as it was." If there be those who would not save the Union, unless they could at the same time *save* slavery, I do not agree with them. If there be those who would not save the Union unless they could at the same time *destroy* slavery, I do not agree with them. My paramount object in this struggle *is* to save the Union, and is *not* either to save or to destroy slavery. If I could save the Union without freeing *any* slave I would do it, and if I could save it by freeing *all* the slaves I would do it; and if I could save it by freeing some and leaving others alone I would also do that. What I do about slavery, and the colored race, I do because I believe it helps to save the Union; and what I forbear, I forbear because I do *not* believe it would help to save the Union. I shall do *less* whenever I shall believe what I am doing hurts the cause, and I shall do *more* whenever I shall believe doing more will help the cause. I shall try to correct errors when shown to be errors; and I shall adopt new views so fast as they shall appear to be true views."[148]

Clearly, his comments supported the belief that Blacks were inferior to Whites. I trust that every Black person would find these comments racist. Does this mean that he was wrong to sign the amendment that freed the slaves? Obviously, this is much more complicated than it seems on the surface.

Next, I think it would be beneficial for Blacks to join the Republican Party, even if the party is full of racist, to negate racism. There has always been racism and there is still racism today. But who would contest the fact that we've made great strides against it? Getting from slavery to where we are now was a struggle and was achieved through a combination of vigilant Blacks who decided they were no longer going to take it and took a stand, and strong, sympathetic Whites who knew what was right. They all sacrificed everything for progress. The next phase is the Republican Party.

If the Republican Party is the last bastion of racism, why not fight to stamp it out? Joining the Republican Party would allow Blacks to dilute the party's alleged racism and force much needed inclusion. Just as the people joined the Freedom Riders during the Civil Rights Movement, we need to join the Republican Party and use our voting power to minimize racism.

Moving beyond racism, Blacks need Republicans because they share core values. It has already been established that Blacks are as evangelical as Republicans and therefore more in line with their values. Many Blacks who are Democrats think Republicans are racist and have never voted Republican; however, they are pro-life, disagree with the DREAM Act, and are opposed to gay marriage. They don't think the Democrats are doing a good job. They feel the government is too big, and they are adamant about their right to own a gun. Some understand that when they vote Democratic they are voting against these beliefs. I've mentioned this to some of them and they say, "I know, but what is my alternative — vote for a racist?" Blacks who are Conservative need to be able to vote for the party with whom they share beliefs.

Morally Acceptable or Morally Wrong, by Party ID

% Morally acceptable

	All Democrats	Nonblack Democrats	Black Democrats	Independents	Republicans
	%	%	%	%	%
Having baby outside of marriage	59	64	38	60	39
Homosexual relations	55	61	31	52	30
Abortion	51	54	37	44	25
Death penalty	57	59	47	65	80
Sex between an unmarried man and woman	64	68	46	66	46
Stem cell research using human embryos	72	76	56	63	48
Should marriages between same-sex couples be recognized by law as valid? (% Yes)	52	57	30	47	22

Frank Newport, "Blacks as Conservative as Republicans on Some Moral Issues", Gallop, 12/3/08

If you look at all of the percentages listed above, Blacks are more in line with Republicans on all except the death penalty, and that is not because of the moral issue. Many Blacks believe in the concept of the death penalty but are concerned about the application of it. In the past, it has been disproportionately used to execute Black offenders. Couple this with innocent people being coerced into confessions and DNA overturning convictions, and Blacks have real fear and concerns with the fairness of it. That being said, with all the other items in the poll, Blacks are consistent with Republicans. In fact, many of them are to the Right of myself on most social issues. Yet they continue to blindly vote for Democrats.

202

The Democrats do a great job of saying what we want to hear. They talk about helping minorities and helping the poor, and we buy into it year after year. There is no evidence that they are any more focused on the Black community than Republicans, but let's assume they are. What if they have good intentions but they're wrong? This leads us to my next reason Blacks should join the Republican Party — for a contingency plan.

It is universally believed that you should diversify your investments, keep batteries and candles around in case of blackouts, and keep safety equipment and blankets in the car in case it breaks down, but for something this important, Blacks don't follow this same logic or heed the words of Dr. Woodson. With all of our proverbial eggs in the Democratic basket, what if their policies don't work?

After FDR took office, the majority of the Black vote swung from the Republicans to the Democrats, but Republicans still got a sizable portion of the Black vote. This all changed with LBJ. Much of this obviously had to do with his 'Great Society'. These programs, unlike Roosevelt's New Deal, were designed specifically to assist the poor and minorities. Even if we assume positive intent, though some supported the program because they expected it to fail, does that mean it worked? Even proponents would have to concede that there were unintended side effects that were detrimental.

Everyone knows that Blacks were poorer, endured more racial injustice, and were less educated prior to the Great Society than they have been since. Yet, the Black family unit was much stronger before than after. In 1968, 4.1% of families were headed by a woman receiving Welfare assistance; in 2011, that number grew to nearly 35%.[149]

While the effects on the Black family are bad, there is also no evidence that the programs have been successful. Poverty, lack of quality education, and crime are worse today than they were in 1964, especially in the Black community. It can be debated whether the programs were a help or hindrance. The bottom line is that we've been following these social policies for 80 years, and it's been 48 years since the Great Society, so isn't it time to at least be open to alternatives?

Change is hard, but the longer we wait to try new ideas, the further down the wrong road we may be going. Perhaps the best plans will come from a combination of Democratic and Republican ideas, but if we ignore everything the Republicans say, our options are limited.

There are also the problems involved with being late to the party. It's long been said that the Republican Party is too White, but in addition to them being open to minorities, we need to be willing to go. If we decided that we should join the Republican Party, then we are going to want to be part of their leadership. Unfortunately, the current leadership will be reluctant to give up power, especially to newcomers. It took decades for Blacks to get seats at the table in the Democratic Party. The longer we wait to join the party, the longer it will take to become part of the decision makers within the party.

Speaking of progress, the Republican Party does a better job on race even with the label of 'racist' as an albatross around their necks. There is no doubt that the Democrats do a better job of talking about race but that the Republicans actually do more, not only in their policies but also with their candidates and appointments. Here are a few surprising facts. First, let's take a look at minority appointments to cabinet positions by party.

Minorities in Presidential Cabinet
(by Party)

	Obama	Clinton	Bush	First Female Appt.	First Minority Appt.
State	D - Hillary Clinton	D - Madeleine Albright	R - Colin Powell R - Condoleeza Rice		R - Colin Powell
Tresury					
Defense					
Justice	D - Eric Holder	D - Janet Reno	R - Alberto Gonzalez		
Interior			R - Gale Ann Norton		
Agriculture		D - Mike Espy	R - Ann Veneman		
Commerce		D - Ron Brown	R - Carlos Gutierrez	D - Juanita Kreps	
Labor	D - Hilda Solis		R - Elaine Chao	D - Frances Perkins	
HHS	D - Kathleen Sebelius			D - Patricia Harris	R - Louis Sullivan
HUD			R - Alphonso Jackson R - Mel Martinez	R - Carla Anderson Hills	R - Samuel Pierce
Transportation		D - Rodney Slater	R - Norman Mineta R - Mary Peters	R - Elizabeth Dole	
Energy	D - Steven Chu	D - Hazel O'Leary D - Federico Pena D - Bill Richardson			
Education			R - Roderick Paige R - Margaret Spellings	D - Shirley Hufstedler	R - Lauro Cavazos
Veteran Affairs	D - Eric Shineski	D - Jesse Brown D - Togo D. West, Jr.			
Homeland Security	D - Janet Napolitano				
EPA	D - Lisa P. Jackson		R - Christine Todd Whitman	R - Anne Gorsuch	
Trade	D - Ron Kirk	D - Charlene Barshefsky	R - Susan Schwab	R - Carla A. Hills	
Un Ambassador	D - Susan Rice			R - Jeane Kirkpatrick	

The chart represents all of the minority and female appointees, with a focus on the last three presidents, since that is when most minorities were appointed. For the positions where the first minority was appointed prior to them, the first appointee is listed followed by the initials of the president who appointed them. Finally, they are color coded by party, blue for Democrats and red for Republicans.

Looking at the chart, you notice that the appointments were pretty even: 24 appointments by Democrats and 23 appointments by Republicans. Also, of the positions whose first appointee came before Clinton, five of the nine women and all three of the minorities were appointed by Republicans.

Next we move to elected officials. We currently have 11 minority governors, eight of them Republicans and three of them Democrats. In the Senate there are 21 minority senators, 11 Democrats and 6 Republicans. We also have to keep in mind that since Blacks vote almost exclusively for Democrats, these minority Republican candidates could not rely on the Black vote to win. Imagine what the Republican Party could do if they had Black support.

One of the first things I realized when I started to pay attention to politics, and one point I continue to make, is that Blacks are diminishing their voting power by giving their vote away. This leads to my next point: Joining the Republican Party will strengthen the Black vote.

Blacks represent approximately 13% of the population, and when we vote in the same direction we have tremendous political power. Unfortunately, we lose much of that power when the Democrats know they can do nothing and still get at least 80% of our vote. They have no vested interest in focusing on the needs of the Black community, so they spend their money and effort wooing other demographics of voters.

Taking the Republican candidates seriously and making both parties earn our vote will give us more choices and give us leverage when the Democrats don't follow through on promises. It's the checks that keep everything balanced. If a politician knows he doesn't have to focus on our needs to get our vote, he won't. There are no checks in this situation, so there will never be balance.

Voting solely for Democrats also affects how we are represented on a state level. Most Blacks live in heavily Democratic areas, but with 30 of the states represented by Republican governors, not all of us live in Democratic controlled states. Often, we will elect Democratic politicians, and when they go to the state capital they can't get anything done. They end up giving in to the more powerful Republican Party. When we have an important issue we want to have addressed, we have no political capital within the Republican Party. Since the state government drives most of the policy choices within the state, Blacks in Atlanta, New Orleans, Houston, and Phoenix need an advocate at the state level.

Blacks need significant representation in the Republican Party. We have a two-party system, so it is illogical not to have representation in both. We've established that both parties have members who are rich and poor, pretty and grotesque, evil and saintly, benevolent and greedy, optimistic and misanthropic, etc. Any categories you can put people in are represented in both parties, with the exception of the Black race. When we give our vote to Democrats exclusively, we weaken our vote, limit our growth, vote against our own values, do nothing to combat racism, and close ourselves to alternative ideas that could possibly help us.

207

Where the Party
Should Go?

Republicans believe that this is a center-Right country; Democrats believe it's center-Left. They're both right — it's just center. While more people identify themselves as Democrats than do Republicans, the total for both only adds up to about 65% of voters. Which way the country breaks depends on how effective the parties are at moving the remaining 35% of the voters. The Republican's ideas appeal more to the majority, but the communication of those ideas and their image is atrocious. The Democrats have better packaging and a better ground game. Unfortunately there is no contest; packaging trumps substance every time.

The first thing Republicans need to do is try to dispel the misconceptions that presently exist. They have to understand that they have a perception problem. In addition to the misconceptions I mentioned earlier in the book, Republicans are perceived as having no empathy or being unsympathetic toward those who are in need. Whether this is true or not, how many people automatically believe this, and how many of them will research the validity of the information? Because of this, Republicans need to understand that they will have to do some things that Democrats just don't have to do.

In order to be effective, this has to be done on a local and national level. Nationally, there needs to be a few people who will serve as advocates whose sole mission will be to address these unfair beliefs. If policy issues are forced into the conversation, I will discuss later how that should be handled. It should be brought back to disproving the misconceptions. These 'advocates' should be made up of a mix of ages, races, and income levels, but they must include at least two high-profile White Republicans. It cannot come off as if they are just using young people and minorities to make them look good.

From a local standpoint, I ask, "What do they do?" I live in Chicago which is a dominantly Democratic area, but there are a small number of Republicans. I would like to see them do the same thing on the local level. I mean, there should be small parties or group discussions where they talk about these misconceptions openly, with no fights over the issues, just discussions about why people believe the misconceptions and how it's impossible for them to be true. Here's a simple start; have book club meetings on this book (Insert shameless plug.). It can help guide the conversation. The Republicans can't continue to ignore certain segments of the population or only have the rich and successful members advocate for the party.

Reince Priebus should take this book and, with a panel of prominent Republicans, schedule a series of town hall events combined with TV shows willing to have them, and have a serious open discussion about race, class, and both political parties.

Republican senators and governors need to have quarterly chats as well. Everyone needs to feel that the Republicans are interested in their needs.

The recent election plays a part in how this will be perceived. Had Romney won, Republicans would have falsely thought that things were okay and that there was no need to invest time and effort in what I'm saying — a bad move since the population is still not changing in their favor, but now with President Obama winning a second term, they will seem to be doing it out of desperation. Either way, this needs to be done to move the Republican Party forward.

Once the groundwork has been laid to create opportunities to dispel the misconceptions, the most important part starts — what to say. There needs to be an open and direct conversation about them, starting with the most damaging — racism.

Not only is this the most damaging, but it's also the hardest to combat, though there are things the Republicans can do. They must first admit that there are racists among them, and while they can't control the voters, they must commit to rooting out the racists within their party. This starts by denouncing extreme actions and comments by party members.

When Akin and Mourdock made their comments about rape and pregnancy regarding abortion, several Republicans denounced their comments, and most of them, along with the Conservative pundits, publicly called for them to resign their campaigns. This is the same reaction they should have when any Conservative makes extreme comments, swift and decisive. Unfortunately, most racism doesn't happen openly anymore; it operates in the shadows. This is where the dialogue becomes extremely important. Republicans need to make a direct appeal to Blacks.

They need to go to community leaders and the Black community to express their sincerity in developing a relationship and having discussions about their needs and the issues important to them. When disagreements arise, they need to be able to explain the reason why their ideas differ and show that it is not based on race.

When it comes to the other misconceptions, the approach should be the same, open and direct. With regard to the Republicans being rich, they should first point out that there are many people in both parties who are rich and that it's unfair to imply that it's only Republicans who are rich. Questioning the wealth of politicians isn't really fair, unless they made their wealth from the taxpayers. Rich people suffer less in bad economies and gain more in good economies than average Americans or the poor. They are simply starting from a better position. There is no need for any wealthy person, Democrat or Republican, to run for political office just to help rich people. They run because they have a desire to give back to their country, and because they have different methods shouldn't change the fact that they have the same intent.

It can be said that some people run for office for the paycheck. The average yearly salary of a rank and file member of Congress is $174,000. It wouldn't be surprising to find that this is more of a motivator for some than giving back, but for the wealthy, this is a huge pay cut.

The Republican approach on social issues has been their Achilles heel, and with the level of passion on both sides, this has hurt them and made them look uncompromising. They need to create a message of fairness stating that regardless of their personal views they will govern based on the Constitution.

212

They also need to clearly state, issue by issue, what their stance is and why, showing how their opponents have distorted their views. While many will still disagree with them, they will understand that the Republicans are not the extremists they've been portrayed to be.

Here's an example of how Republicans should address a polarizing social issue, abortion. When Republicans got together to propose defunding Planned Parenthood, a firestorm was started. Republicans came off, once again, looking like the uncaring group who were trying to control women's bodies, and the "War on Women" attacks began. This is what they should have said. If they speak like this, they will seem less extreme:

"While the majority of the party thinks that abortion is bad and should be limited as much as possible, we understand that it is the law of the land and we have no plans to overturn Roe v. Wade. However, just as we need to respect the fact the many believe this is a viable option, the obligation of all politicians is to govern the entire population, fairly. There is a large population of evangelicals who have a strong moral objection to abortion. We have to consider their concerns as well. We cannot and should not stop women from exercising their rights because of other's views; however, in the same spirit of compromise, proponents of these rights must understand that we cannot and should not allow tax dollars to pay for these services. This is the reason we oppose the funding to Planned Parenthood. It is not because we are trying to stop them from performing abortions, nor are we trying to imply that this is the bulk of the services they provide. We are open to discussing some alternative ways to address this issue, and though many will still disagree with us, you can't believe that our purpose is to limit women's rights or control their bodies. In the 40 years since Roe v Wade, Republicans have been president for 24 of those years, including the year it was decided, and the Supreme Court has been headed by a Republican appointee all of those years, yet no attempts to change the law have been made. There is a law against funding abortions with tax dollars, and since Planned Parenthood accepts federal funding, it is our obligation to ensure that these funds are not being used for this purpose. If Planned Parenthood did not accept federal funds, we would not have an objection to their services."

The next thing Republicans need to do is recruit minorities. The population is growing, and the fastest growing groups in America are Blacks and Hispanics who currently make up about 25% of the population and are more likely to vote Democratic. While the reasons are similar for both groups, the effect is much greater with Blacks than with Hispanics. In 2008, John McCain got 31% of the Hispanic vote and 4% of the Black vote. While having the first non-White candidate in the general election surely had an effect on the Black vote, John Kerry got 88% of the Black vote in 2004, which was down from the 90% Al Gore got in 2000.

Republicans have to make an attempt to attract these minority voters. As hard-fought as campaigns are and as close as the outcomes can be, they can't afford to have 15% of the population voting against them automatically. A lot of the changes in their voting habits will have to come from the Blacks themselves. They will have to look at the issues and decide which candidate is better; however, changing the fact that they won't listen to what Republicans say has to be addressed by both sides. It can start with the Republicans' attempt to remove the racist label.

214

This racist label was given to them through a slow and methodical smear campaign by the Democratic Party. The Republicans, however, have done very little to combat that label. The primary issue is that it is hard to prove a negative. You can accuse someone of being a racist without having any proof and people will take it as fact. Proving you're *not* a racist is not as easy. If someone calls you a racist, you can't just pull out your 'I'm not a racist' registration card.

This is one of the reasons I think calling someone a racist is one of the worst things to do. It's character assassination. Once you're labeled a racist, everyone believes it to be true. There's no trial, no evidentiary hearing. Even if there's no evidence of racism and somehow you're deemed not to be a racist, nothing happens to the person who accused you of it.

Republicans need Blacks to help eliminate these labels. They can't prove they're not racists from afar. They need to be amongst Blacks to build a foundation with them. This is the same for all minorities. Republicans need a broader representation within the party.

Diversity is a great advantage that Democrats have over Republicans, and the Republicans need to bridge that gap. As in business, education, and other arenas, diversity is key to growth and development. This is no different in politics. Having a diverse group of decision makers creates new ideas and gives new perspective to problems, since different groups have different views and different problems. Republicans cannot get a diverse group of decision makers in the party if they only have White men from whom to pick.

Republicans need Blacks because they share ideas and values. As we established earlier, many Blacks have Conservative ideas and values, but they vote for the other party. The Republicans cannot afford to lose the vote of like-minded constituents, and having more people in their party strengthens their message.

Lastly, Republicans need Blacks because it's right. You can't want to represent the majority of the country when you have around 5% of Blacks and 30% of Hispanics. The party cannot succeed when a large percentage of the population defaults to the other party. Republicans also cannot be the party for everyone when they don't have everyone in their party, especially when their opponent has representation from all groups.

Throughout this book I have spoken specifically about Blacks and the Republican Party. This is because the Black vote is the most disparate of the various demographics and the group with which I have first-hand knowledge. However, these points can be applied across all demographics. Republicans need to focus on inclusion of the Hispanic and LGBT communities. Throughout this year's campaign, some Republicans continue to use rhetoric that is insensitive to Hispanics and limited to the gay community, yet they will no doubt get more votes from these communities than from Blacks. This proves that there is an element of the population who believe in smaller government and greater freedom in every group. Therefore, Republicans need to stop talking about the deportation of illegals, which we all know will never happen, and limiting gay rights, which adds regulation and is against their core beliefs.

Conservatives in these groups, such as Black Conservatives, need to communicate their views to their communities as well as work together to collectively bring minority issues to the leadership of the Republican Party. Instead of having several Conservative groups focusing on different priorities, minorities

216

within the party need to develop one voice. This will result in much better communication to the leadership of the party as well as a more cohesive message to their communities. The Log Cabin Republicans, the National Black Republican Association, the Republican National Hispanic Assembly, and other minority groups within the Conservative movement must work together to maximize their impact.

Once the Republicans have addressed the misconceptions and broadened their overall appeal, they can focus on the last two phases of moving the party forward, adjusting the way they campaign, and refining how they communicate their stance on the issues.

The first step is to minimize the anger. Being mean turns people off. It also makes you look as if you are trying too hard and so you must have an ulterior motive. This is why when the Republicans attacked Clinton he won the second term in a landslide. When Democrats attacked Bush, he won a second term even though we were told he stole the first one. Attacking Obama will hurt the Republican Party as well.

Republicans need to focus on why they are right and spend less time painting a negative picture of Democrats. People need a clear choice from both parties and need to see where they differ. They can then choose the party whose views they support. The Republicans should create ads that simply talk about the positives of Conservatism with no comments about the Democratic Party.

Next, Republicans need to increase their visibility in areas that are heavily Democratic. As I stated earlier, I grew up in an area where Republicans were virtually extinct. Though I understand that elections are costly, there is also a great cost to simply

217

conceding elections. Having both parties represented in local and statewide elections gives everyone an idea of what the parties' beliefs are. It is also easier for people to believe misconceptions about Republicans when there are no party members around to refute these views. They cannot continue to win heavily Republican areas 70/30 but lose Democratic areas 85/15, especially since these Democratic areas have larger populations.

As Republicans strive for broader appeal, they cannot leave out the Libertarians. They have to find a way to get them to blend into the Republican Party instead of them voting for the Libertarian candidate. In the late 1990s, I thought having a 3rd party was a good idea. The Democrats had failed me and the Republicans had ignored me. I even voted for a 3rd party candidate in 2000. I didn't realize the impact this had at the time and neither do the members of the Libertarian Party.

Most of them primarily identify with Republicans. They want a smaller federal government and one that follows the Constitution. Most are willing to go to the point of reversing powers they feel the federal government has assumed but are not given them by the Constitution. While they may be right about some of these, it's impossible to unring the bell. This is why every presidential candidate who talks about repealing something loses. Libertarians are really upset because the Republicans don't practice what they preach and grow the government just like the Democrats do.

Libertarians believe their views on social issues are different as well. Most of them don't really care what others do. Many endorse legalizing what they call victimless crimes, such as drugs and prostitution. Like the other social Liberals, Republicans need to let them know that they are not interested in legislating social issues, or, at the very least, that they are willing to have *some* varying opinions within the party.

Republicans need to let the Libertarians know that they are only serving to assist the Democrats by voting for a third party candidate or by not voting at all. The third party plan cannot work. We have a hard enough time choosing a candidate now. Do we really want to have someone win the election with 40% of the vote? Like it or not, it's much better when the winner actually gets at least half of the votes.

Republicans must change the way they address sensitive issues. It doesn't matter if you are right if you come off as unsympathetic. You can't attack ideas that make people feel good, even if the ideas are bad. If the Republicans, for example, decide that it would be a bad idea to extend unemployment benefits, they have to temper their message so that it doesn't come off as them having no empathy for people who have been unemployed for an extended period of time. Even if extending the benefits would be bad for the economy, why would anyone struggling with long-term unemployment vote for someone who tried to cancel their benefits.

I guess what I'm saying is that Republicans need to be more sensitive when conveying their message. They need to understand that *how* the message is delivered is as important as the message itself. They need to stop saying things such as, "Pull yourself up by your bootstraps." Most people hear this and think, "What happens to those who can't succeed by pulling themselves up, not to mention the people who don't have boots let alone bootstraps?" Republicans have to realize that what they say is not what people hear.

I mentioned earlier that Republicans would have to do some things that Democrats are not doing; one is to stop using lies and confusion to advance their agenda. While both parties do this, the Democrats have the advantage of people actually believing their lies and confusion and the media to help them spread it. Republicans don't have that luxury in such large numbers.

If the Republicans believe that raising taxes on the rich won't help the economy, then they need to find a better way to convey that message. They went with the "Raising taxes will limit job growth" instead of simply saying that it's wrong, that it won't raise enough revenue to affect the deficit, and that it's never a good idea to raise taxes in a bad economy. The job growth comment was a better way to scare people into reacting; however, it wasn't completely true. They need to set a standard for themselves above that which the other party currently sets for themselves. They need to draft comments that are fact-check proof. Using half-truths to make your point just seems deceptive, and since the Republicans are the party with the perception problem, this can only hurt them.

The way I see it, both parties need to get rid of the rhetoric and stand by their beliefs alone. They both believe they have the best interest of the country in mind. Just give the people enough information, honestly, and let them decide. This brings us to the issues themselves.

There needs to be an open and honest dialog with voters where Republicans repeat this basic message over and over: "We agree with the Democrats on the importance of many issues; we just differ in the methods to improve them. While there are bad apples in every bunch, and this goes for our party as well as the

220

Democrats, you have to believe that we both share the goal of improving the country."

Once we get past the misconceptions and focus on the real issues that plague our country, Republicans must focus on the fundamental differences between the two parties, not the issue-by-issue fight. No one will agree with either party on every issue, and there will always be blurry lines within each party on any given issue, but they will agree on the basic differences that separate the parties.

The Democrats believe that the government should be the primary arbiter to help those who need it and that the help should come in the form of policies that address the specific needs and/or problems of a niche group (Blacks, Hispanics, women, the poor, etc.). The Republicans believe that the government does have an important stake in helping these groups but that their help should be ancillary to the help of private businesses, charities, and the people themselves. Also, from a policy standpoint, Republicans believe that the government should create policies that help the greatest number of people and not separate policies depending on the group.

There are two problems with the Democrats' plan. The first is that there is no way to effectively create policies targeted to one group. The members of any given group won't have the same socioeconomic status, views on issues, or be in the same geographical area. Due to these complexities, there's no plan that could help the entire group.

The second problem is logical; it's simply not the best way to help. Even if you believe that it's the government's job to create these plans, there's no historic evidence that they are capable of

221

doing so. There's a limit to how much revenue the government gets, so when money is slated for a specific group, it has to be taken from somewhere else. This has the potential of creating animosity toward the group who is getting policies tailored to their needs.

There is also the problem of implementation. All of us have first-hand experience in dealing with bureaucratic red tape. We know the government is not the most efficient organization when it comes to operating within a budget or timeframe. Additionally, the federal government is so large that it makes it difficult to truly understand the specific needs of communities or neighborhoods. If they have historically failed at everything they tried to manage, then why give them more money and greater controls?

Then there's the corruption. Let me say that this is not party specific, nor is it the norm. Corruption happens on both sides, and while it probably isn't as prevalent as it seems, it's not exactly rare. We constantly hear stories of politicians using campaign dollars and tax funds to buy property, take trips, and give businessmen favors. While we can't completely eliminate corruption, giving the politicians a bigger budget will only make matters worse.

In addition to this type of outright corruption, which may be infrequent, there is the everyday wheeling and dealing done by almost all politicians, which at best bogs down operations and costs the taxpayers money and at worst is corrupt in a different way, causing their constituents to lose out on their needs to the betterment of the federal agenda.

The Republicans believe that the government's role should be derived from the Constitution and that the current government format has moved too far away from the constitutional framework, yet they have no problem taking advantage of it. They also believe that the government should be focused on legislation that benefits the greatest number of people instead of specific groups. Not only is this the most effective method, but it's fair for everyone. As opposed to tailoring help to these groups, helping the majority of people will leave fewer people in need. Once this has been established, they can focus on helping those who need it.

While the Republicans believe that the federal government has become too large, they do agree that the government has a responsibility to help those in need. Where they disagree with the Democrats is the method and the amount of the help.

Since they have a greater focus on limiting the federal government, the Republicans believe that the local government is in a better position to understand the needs of its community. This is where government help should begin. When the local government has maximized its resources, the state government should supply assistance. If the state government cannot meet those needs, only then should the federal government supplement some of the costs. This is the opposite of the Democrats' method.

A more glaring difference is that the Republicans believe the government should be the second line of assistance for those who need help. The first should be the many non-profits that specialize in helping those with specific needs. Whether it be feeding the hungry, job training, or housing, these charitable organizations do a tremendous job of helping those in need and are uniquely equipped to understand the best way to maximize their efforts.

In addition to non-profits, the local businesses in the community can add valuable assistance to complement them. Many people set aside a portion of their income to donate to those

223

in need. Like the hundreds of millions of dollars donated by the wealthy, many corporations look for ways to give back to the community. The government should work as a liaison between these organizations who are offering support, rather than using tax dollars as the primary source of funding. I know that many people believe corporations are evil. I'm not naïve enough to believe that all corporations are overtly benevolent, but I believe most would be inclined to help. Since corporations are concerned about how they're viewed in society, they want to be known as part of the community. There are also tax incentives that will motivate them to offer these services.

The Republican Party has traditionally been the party of ideas and needs to become that again. While not all of their ideas will be popular and some won't work, they have to show that they care and that they just want to find the most successful plan. They need to suggest other ways to do things, such as the example above to help the poor, and they need to explain that these ways are designed to minimize the cost to taxpayers while getting the necessary results. They must be specific and remind people that having good intentions is not enough; you have to implement the right plans.

When Republicans disagree with a proposal by Democrats, they need to offer an alternative. You can't be a leader simply by saying your opponent is wrong. They need to explain why their opponent is wrong, offer an alternative, and do it while showing empathy for those suffering from the problem. They also have to show why reliance on the government is bad for everyone. Everyone knows that the government can be slow, inefficient, and lacking when it comes to providing help for its constituents. When

224

you factor in political favors and corruption, it's clear why giving them more money is not the answer. There is also something to be said for creating your own success and not having to follow the rules and limitations that come with getting government help.

Republicans need to take these suggestions seriously and start to implement them. This will help them make inroads with the groups who they have a hard time reaching. Blacks need to realize that not all Republicans are racist and that they don't all have ulterior motives. Blacks also need to understand that not everything that sounds good is going to be beneficial. At the end of the day, if Republicans can start to speak openly and honestly to all groups and if Blacks can set aside their emotions, listen attentively, and use logic to make decisions, everybody's chances improve.

False Assumptions
of the Election Results

I finished the book just before the 2012 election, so I wasn't able to consider the results. After the election, there was a lot of glee from Democrats and a lot of paranoia from Republicans. This was to be expected. Most of the talk was about why Obama won and what the Republican Party needed to do to recover. After listening to varying opinions, I thought about editing the book to add my comments on the results but realized that I had already written specific details about how different groups vote and the problem Republicans would have. I decided to address the results because I thought the political analysts and reporters were wrong, or at least shortsighted in their analysis.

I'm not saying that they were wrong in describing how people voted. Their analysis of the different demographic groups and how they voted was generally accurate. What I disagreed with was the reason they believed certain groups voted the way they did and what it means for the country.

Both sides seem to agree that the 2012 election marked a shift in the ideology of the county. The Democrats believe it was a mandate, stating that their views on the issues were correct, while Republicans believed that the country took a permanent shift to the Left. I will explain why both of these arguments are incorrect.

While there may have been a slight shift to the Left, this is neither permanent nor a sign of things to come. Things tend to sway back and forth after a couple of election cycles. The Democrats were fearful when they lost control of Congress in 1994. In 2004, after seeing Bush "steal" the 2000 election, they were all but certain they would get the White House back. After their shocking loss, they wondered what they had done wrong. Again, in 2010, Republicans gained control of the House of Representatives, and Obama called it, in a word, "Humbling". So now it's the Republicans' turn to be humbled, and while they are licking their wounds and the Democrats are riding high, I believe both parties are premature in their assertions. Let's take a look at the results.[150]

I listened to a week of Republican after Republican stating how we are now an entitlement country. The Conservative journalists and talk radio hosts believed that Obama won because he offered people "free stuff", and they are not alone. In a private conversation a week after the election, Romney told donors, "It's a proven political strategy, which is, give a bunch of money from the government to a group, and guess what? They vote for you." He was implying that President Obama won because of "gifts" he'd given to certain groups. While for many this came off as insensitive, racist, and only exacerbated the negative perceptions I've mentioned that Republicans have, I want to deal with the more important problem; the fact that he is wrong.

There are, no doubt, millions of Americans who will take advantage of these government entitlements if they are available.

228

I also agree that many of these Americans voted for Obama, though not at the level the Republicans would like you to believe. However, in order for this to be the source of Obama's victory, a large number of people who won't be eligible for entitlements must have voted for him as well. People making at least $50,000 make up 59% of the electorate. Romney would have easily won if he could have dominated this demographic at the same rate Obama dominated the "entitlement society". While Romney did win this group, he only won by 8%, not enough to offset the 22% disadvantage he had among those making less than $50,000. And while many falsely believe wealthy Americans are all Republicans, Obama beat Romney amongst those making the most money. In fact, he won in 8 of the 10 wealthiest counties in America. These are the people who will be footing the bill for the entitlements, but they still voted for Obama. As for those in the bottom third, Romney got 38% of their vote — not high enough but enough to say that the majority weren't voting for free stuff. So saying people voted for Obama to get free stuff is an oversimplification.

Next comes the 'blame the candidate' phase of the analysis. This is common in any loss. They ask, "What did our candidate do wrong?" and not, "What did our opponents do right?" They went through their list: Romney didn't carry the aggression of the first debate through the other debates; his comments on the 47% and self-deportation hurt him, and Hurricane Sandy helped Obama. Then it came to his position as a Conservative. Some said that he was too moderate and that the base wouldn't support him, while others said that the party needed to shift to a more moderate stance to include more people. They continue to miss the point.

There are many things that affect an election, and several of them may have attributed to Romney's loss, but one thing's for sure, he did not lose because of the issues. Bill O'Reilly was one of those who talked about the entitlement issue, but I must admit that he did the best job of trying to determine why people voted for Obama. While questioning a pundit from each party, he asked each of them to tell him specifically what the people voted for. When they veered away from the question to the party talking points, he cut them off and asked them to give him a simple answer. Neither guest could do it. I will answer him; they weren't voting for *anything*. If you want to know what they voted for, go back and read chapter 13, how we elect presidents. I will continue to say, the sooner the Republicans learn how to play the game, the sooner they can make a real attempt to win. Obviously, Republicans must have a clear direction for the party, but they must also face the truth. While entitlements that were offered played a small role in President Obama's re-election, the three primary reasons Romney lost are: Race, Perception, and Message.

We all know that race is a problem, but no one has actually looked down that rabbit hole to see just how deeply it goes. The pundits on both sides are very intelligent people, far more educated than I am, and evaluating election results is what they do. Yet in all the coverage I listened to, no one mentioned anything about race. This is because we still can't have an open conversation about race. Since Obama won the Democrat nomination in 2008, there have been several districts in Atlanta, Chicago, Cleveland, and Philadelphia where the Republican candidate, in both presidential elections, got zero votes.[151] [152] Are you going to tell me that this has nothing to do with race? Some Republicans will say that this proves there was voter fraud, while most Democrats will disagree.

230

But it has to be one or the other. Either there was voter fraud or race played a large part in how people voted. And yes, there are racists who voted against Obama solely due to race, but the number of people who came out to vote for Obama due to race far outnumbered those who voted against him for the same reason.

It's easy to see that many were motivated by race. People who use logic will vary their preferences based on the issues that are important to them, but no matter what their leaning, Romney got at least 20% of the vote of every demographic. He got 22% of gays and lesbians, 37% of voters who want to see citizenship extended to illegals, 31% of unmarried women, and so on. No matter how the country is divided or what demographic you look at, Romney was able to reach a portion of that demographic except for Blacks.[153] Needless to say, because of these strong views on race, many are afraid to say what they believe for fear they will be called a racist. This is the reason none of the political analysts mentioned race as an issue. This does nothing to advance race relations. I think everyone should say what they feel. In any event, this rationale was completely overlooked.

Another topic that I mentioned throughout the book that was an issue for the Romney campaign was the Republicans' negative perception. For Blacks, this has been the perception of Republicans ever since Johnson's 'Great Society'. In this election cycle, however, Democrats were able to extend that negative perception to women and Hispanics. The "War on Women" rhetoric caused people to vote *against* Republicans rather than *for* Obama. The election was thought to be about the economy, and if it was, Romney would have won. Many minority and women voters decided to vote for Obama regardless of their views for fear of what the Republicans would do. Here is my best example of how powerful these perceptions are and why I believe most people don't vote on issues: When asked the question, "What is the most important candidate quality," Romney wins all categories except "Cares about people". So even though they believe Romney has a vision for the country and is a stronger leader than Obama, they didn't vote for him because the perception is that he doesn't care, and who wants a president who doesn't care? Perception is a major problem for Republicans and, unlike the race factor, was given some attention in the post-election analysis, but it had a greater impact on the election than entitlements.

Most Important Candidate Quality

	% of voters	Obama	Romney
Shares my values	27%	42	55
Strong Leader	18%	38	61
Vision for future	29%	45	54
Cares about people	21%	81	18

The third and final reason Romney lost is the message, or better, how the message was delivered. If the race issue gave the Democrats the Blacks, and the "War on Women" gave them the edge among women, the way the Republicans delivered their message pushed everyone further toward Obama. Romney's comments about 47% of the population alienated poor people, while the comments of Senators Akins and Mourdock gave credence to the perception that Republicans want to control women's bodies, and stances against immigration reform lost much of the Hispanic vote. I won't go into too much detail with this one because everyone agrees that the message needs to be improved. Republicans need to use this book as a guide to framing that message.

Taking the election as a whole, Romney did not lose as badly as people are describing. Remember, Romney lost the popular vote by just over 3%. Obama won 93% of the Black vote, 71% of the Hispanic vote, and 55% of the female vote. This adds up to over 25% of the vote, but Romney only lost by 3%. If Republicans can only learn to get Blacks, Hispanics, and women to *listen,* they can win. Notice, none of these points had anything to do with a shift in ideology, not for the country or for the Republican Party. Another look inside the numbers shows that these groups continue to break the way they always have. The issue becomes turning out the vote. Take voter age, for instance. Young people are traditionally more Liberal. Romney won all age groups from 40 years old to seniors, and, interestingly, the higher the age, the bigger percentage of the vote he got. This is in spite of the attacks on the Republican stance on Social Security. The problem is, he lost the 18 through 39 year olds by a larger gap than he won the older voters. But I ask you, what are the chances that these young voters were basing their votes on clearly defined beliefs and researched issues? My guess is that the chances are very slim.

I believe I have proven that the country didn't make a dramatic shift Left, not because the beliefs of many voters don't lean that way but because they aren't basing their votes on their beliefs. I will end this book the way I started it: in the hopes that I can get more people to use logic in their decision making. Republicans cannot continue to concede 95% of the nation's capital and the Black vote to the Democrats just as Blacks have gone too far by buying into the fear and misconceptions of old. We need to open an honest dialogue on race, and it is imperative that Blacks and Republicans address their issues and keep an open mind for the betterment of the country and the continued advancement of the Republican Party and the Black community as a whole.

Appendix 1 – Illinois Politicians with Criminal Charges

ILLINOIS POLITICIANS	YEAR	POSITION	CHARGES
Convicted			
Tony Peraica	2012	Cook County Commissioner	Ŧ Damaging opponent's yard signs
Isaac Carothers	2010	Alderman	Federal corruption charges
Nicholas Blasé	2010	Mayor of Niles	Mail fraud and tax evasion
Rod Blagojevich	2009	Governor	Extortion
Al Sanchez	2009	Commissioner Streets and Sanitation	Mail fraud
Arenda Troutman	2008	Alderman	Mail fraud and tax fraud
Ed Vrdolyak	2007	Alderman	Conspiracy to commit Mail and wire fraud
Arthur Swanson	2006	Former State Senator	Lying to Grand Jury
James Laski	2006	City Clerk	Extortion/obstruction of justice
John Briatta*	2006	City Employee	Extortion
Daniel Katalinic	2005	Deputy Commissioner Streets and Sanitation	Mail fraud
George Ryan	2003	Governor	Racketeering, conspiracy, and fraud
Betty Loren-Maltese	2002	Cicero Town President	Stole $12MM in insurance scam
Virgil Jones	1999	Alderman	Extortion and tax charges
Percy Giles	1999	Alderman	Racketeering, bribery extortion, and filing false income tax returns
Miriam Santos	1999	City Treasurer	Mail fraud and attempted extortion
Ambrosio Medrano	1995	Alderman	Extortion
Lawrence Bloom	1995	Alderman	Tax fraud
Dan Rostenkowski	1994	Congressman Chairman Ways and Means	Corruption in post office scandal
Mel Reynolds**	1994	Congressman	sexual assault, bank fraud
Walter Kozubowski	1993	City Clerk (Laski's predecessor)	Mail fraud, bank fraud, and tax evasion
David Shields	1992	Cook County Circuit Court Judge	Accepting bribes
Wallace Davis, Jr	1987	Alderman	Extortion and racketeering
Michael McNulty	1987	Cook County Circuit Court Judge	Tax evasion
Martin Tuchow	1985	Cook County Commissioner	Extortion
Pending Cases			
Jessie Jackson, Jr.	2012	U.S. Congressman	Misuse of campaign funds (FBI investigation)
Lashawn Ford	2012	State Senator	Bank fraud (Indicted)
William Beavers	2012	County Commissioner	Tax fraud (on trial)
Donnie Trotter	2012	State Senator	Attempting to board a plane with a gun

* Briatta is the brother-in-law of John Daley (Former White House chief of staff and Mayor Daley's brother)
** Pardoned for bank fraud by President Clinton
Ŧ Misdemeanor

References

1   Brain Dead Burockracy - http://www.myspace.com/brain_dead_burockracy.
2   http://en.wikipedia.org/wiki/Black_sitcom#1990s.
3   Greg Braxton, "Jackson Urges Churches to Protest Oscars", *LA Times*, 3/24/1996, latimes.com.
4   *Mr. T and Tina*, http://www.imdb.com/title/tt0074027/.
5   *All-American Girl*, http://www.imdb.com/title/tt0108693/.
6   "Overview of Race and Hispanic Origin: 2010", *census.gov*, 4.
7   Prisoners in 2010, U.S. Department of Justice, *Bureau of Justice Statistics*, 2/9/12, bjs.ojp.usdoj.gov Table 13, 26.
8   Julian Abagond, "Black People According to American Television", *Wordpress.com*, 2/3/10, abagond.wordpress.com.
9   Race IAT - www.implicit.harvard.edu.
10 Malcolm Gladwell, *Blink: The Power of Thinking Without Thinking*, (Back Bay Books, 2007), 84.
11 Malcolm Gladwell, *Blink: The Power of Thinking Without Thinking*, (Back Bay Books, 2007), 85.
12 Dan Rozek, "Four Charged with Wrigleyville Beatings were Shooting a Rap Video", *Sun Times*, 7/9/2012, www.suntimes.com.
13 Parents Music Resource Center - http://en.wikipedia.org/wiki/Parents_Music_Resource_Center.
14 U.S. Department of Justice, www.amberalert.gov.
15 CBS News, "Experts: Media Biased In Missing Kids Coverage", *CBS News.com*, 10/10/2011, www.cbsnews.com.
16 The Week Editorial Staff, "The Trayvon Martin Case: A Timeline", *The Week*, 07/17/2012, theweek.com.
17 Rene Lynch, "Trayvon Martin case: Rev. Al Sharpton takes civil rights state", *LA Times*, 3/22/12, latimes.com.
18 Newsone staff, "Miami Heat Players Don Hoodies For Trayvon Martin", *Newsone*, 5/24/2012, http://newsone.com/1954635/miami-heat-trayvon-martin/.

19 Michael Pearson, "Gunman turns 'Batman' screening into real-life 'horror film'", *CNN*, 7/20/12, www.cnn.com.

20 Sun-Times Media Wire, "3 Killed, 18 Hurt in shootings Since Friday Night", *CBS Chicago*, 7/21/12, http://chicago.cbslocal.com/2012/07/21/.

21 Sun-Times Media Wire, "436th Homicide, Chicago Surpasses Last Year", *CBS Chicago*, 10/29/12, http://chicago.cbslocal.com/2012/10/29.

22 Crimesider Staff, "Heaven Sutton, 7-year-old Chicago girl, fatally shot moments after getting hair styled for trip to Disney World", *CBS News*, 6/29/12, www.cbsnews.com.

23 Susan Jones, "Chicago Mayor Appeals to Gangsters' 'Values': Get Away From That Kid'", *CNS News*, 7/10/12, www.cnsnews.com.

24 Connections for Abused Women and their Children, www.cawc.org.

25 The Cara Program, www.thecaraprogram.org

26 Merriam-Webster, racism, www.merriam-webster.com.

27 Audarshia Townsend, "Jessica Elizabeth Racist Rant", *(312) Diningdiva*, 3/29/12, 312diningdiva.blogspot.com.

28 Mark Whittington, "James Byrd's Murder Led to More Hate-Crime Laws", *Yahoo News*, 9/22/11, www.news.yahoo.com.

29 Nicola Menzie, "Black Couple Denied Wedding at Miss. Church After White Members 'Pitch a Fit'", *Christian Post*, 7/30/12.

30 "Fisher vs. University of Texas Oral Arguments Transcript", *New York Times*, 10/12/12, www.nytimes.com.

31 Kelley L. Carter, "Etta James Honored at Grammys by Alicia Keys, Bonnie Raitt", *MTV*, 2/12/12, www.mtv.com/news.

32 "Stars to Join for Aretha Franklin Tribute", *Grammy.com*, 2/9/11, www.grammy.com/news.

33 Ron Wynn, "Where's the Black Audience?", *Jazz Times*, Jan/Feb 2003, www.jazztimes.com.

34 Shawnna, Wikipedia, http://en.wikipedia.org/wiki/Shawnna.

35 Frederick Douglass, *My Bondage and My Freedom*, Kindle edition, 218

36 GOP-Our History - www.gop.com.

37 "13th Amendment to the U.S. Constitution: Abolition of Slavery", *National Archives*, www.archives.gov.

38 David Whitney and Robin Vaughn Whitney, *The American Presidents*, (J. G. Ferguson Publishing Company , 1989), 154.

39 Civil Rights Act of 1866 - http://civilrightsactof1866.com/.

40 Grover Cleveland and Civil Rights - potus-geeks.livejournal.com, 10/10/2011

41 Cleveland Signs Chinese Exclusion Act 10/8/1888 - http://millercenter.org/president/events/10_08.

42 "Scott Act 1888", *Encyclopedia of Immigration*, 02/27/2011, http://immigration-online.org.

43 Malcolm A Kine, "Progressive Segregation", *Accuracy in Academia*, 2/28/08, http://www.academia.org.

44 Richard Weingroff, "The Road to Civil Rights Woodrow Wilson", *U.S. Department of Transportation, Highway History*, 4/7/11, http://www.fhwa.dot.gov/highwayhistory/road/s09.cfm.

45 Arthur Link, *Wilson: The Road to the White House* (Princeton University Press, 1947) 502.

46 Jean Edward Smith, "Ku Klux Klan Act", *Grant*, (Simon & Schuster, 2001), 542–547.

47 The Civil Rights Act of March 1, 1875 - http://chnm.gmu.edu/courses/122/recon/civilrightsact.html.

48 15th Amendment to the U.S. Constitution: Voting Rights (1870) - www.ourdocuments.gov

49 James Garfield and Slavery - http://potus-geeks.livejournal.com/161169.html, 10/6/2011.

50 NPR Staff, "Teddy Roosevelt's 'Shocking' Dinner with Washington", *NPR*, 5/14/12, http://www.npr.org/2012/05/14/152684575/teddy-roosevelts-shocking-dinner-with-washington.

51 Andrew Glass, "President Harding condemns lynching, Oct. 21, 1921", *Politico*, 10/21/09, http://www.politico.com.

52 Coolidge Resources - http://www.calvin-coolidge.org/calvin-coolidge-and-race.html

53 The Great Depression and New Deal, 1929-1940s - http://iws.collin.edu/kwilkison/Online1302home/20th%20Century/DepressionNewDeal.html.

54 The New Deal - http://www.u-s-history.com/pages/h1851.html

55 Jim Powell, "Why Did FDR's New Deal Harm Blacks?", *Cato Institute*, 12/3/03, www.cato.org.

56 "Internment History", PBS, www.pbs.org. Accessed May, 12, 2012.

57 Desegregation of the Armed Forces - www.trumanlibrary.org

58 Executive Order 10308 - http://www.presidency.ucsb.edu/ws/index.php?pid=78360, 12/3/1951

59 The 1960 Civil Rights Act - http://www.historylearningsite.co.uk/1960_civil_rights_act.htm

60 Tom Murse, http://usgovinfo.about.com/od/uscongress/tp/Five-Longest-Filibusters.htm

61 Anthony Lewis, "On this Day: President Sends Troops to Little Rock, Federalized Arkansas National Guard; Tells Nation He Acted to Avoid Anarchy", *NY Times*, 9/25/1957, www.nytimes.com.

62 State of the Union Address, Dwight D. Eisenhower, 2/2/1953, http://www.infoplease.com/t/hist/state-of-the-union/165.html

63 Civil Rights Movement - http://www.jfklibrary.org/JFK/JFK-in-History/Civil-Rights-Movement.aspx

64 Richard Reeves, *President Kennedy: Profile of Power*, (Simon and Schuster, 1994), 580-584

65 Jen Christensen, "FBI tracked King's every move", *CNN*, 12/29/2008, www.cnn.com.

66   Civil Rights Act (1964) - http://www.ourdocuments.gov/doc.php?flash=true&doc=97

67   June 10, 1964 Civil Rights Filibuster Ended - http://www.senate.gov/artandhistory/history/minute/Civil_Rights_Filibuster_Ended.htm

68   Civil Rights Act of 1964 roll call vote breakdown by numbers - http://www.waylandsmalley.com/Civil_Rights_Vote.htm

69   Voting Rights Act (1965) - http://www.ourdocuments.gov/doc.php?flash=true&doc=100

70   "People & Events: The 1964 Republican Campaign", *PBS*, www.pbs.org. Accessed May, 12, 2012.

71   Blacks and the Democratic Party - http://factcheck.org/2008/04/Blacks-and-the-democratic-party/

72   Thomas Walker, "US President – D Primaries", *Our Campaigns*, www.ourcampaigns.com

73   Thomas Walker, "US President – R Primaries", *Our Campaigns*, http://www.ourcampaigns.com/RaceDetail.html?RaceID=55211

74   State and Local Tax Policy: What are the sources of revenue for local governments? = http://www.taxpolicycenter.org/briefing-book/state-local/revenues/local_revenue.cfm, pp. 1 & 2

75   Federal Funds and State Fiscal Independence - http://www.heritage.org/research/reports/2008/05/federal-funds-and-state-fiscal-independence, Sven R. Larson, 5/15/2008

76   Thomas Hardy, "Gary Elects Its First White Mayor Since 1967", *Chicago Tribune*, 11/8/95, http://articles.chicagotribune.com.

77   First Black Mayors - http://en.wikipedia.org/wiki/List_of_first_African-American_mayors

78   White House – Rutherford B. Hayes - http://www.Whitehouse.gov/about/presidents/rutherfordbhayes

79   http://www.thegreenpapers.com/News/20000702-0.html

80   Reflections on Presidential Job Approval and Re-election Odds - http://www.gallup.com/poll/8608/Reflections-Presidential-Job-Approval-Reelection-Odds.aspx, Frank Newport, 6/10/2003

81   Voter turnout in the U.S. presidential elections - http://en.wikipedia.org/wiki/Voter_turnout_in_the_United_States_presidential_elections

82   Voter Turnout by country - http://en.wikipedia.org/wiki/Voter_turnout

83   Lisa De Moraes, "Kanye West's Torrent of Criticism, Live on NBC", *Washington Post*, 9/3/05, www.washingtonpost.com.

84   Glenn Kessler, "When did McConnell say he wanted to make Obama a 'one-term president", *the Washington Post*, 9/25/12, http://www.washingtonpost.com/blogs/fact-checker

85   "Transcript of Paul Ryan's speech at RNC", *Fox News*, 8/29/12, www.foxnews.com.

86   Genesis Saboteur, "Barack Obama Speaking at the GM Plant", *youtube*, Video posted on 9/1/12, www.youtube.com.

87   President Bill Clinton at the 2012 Democratic National Convention - http://www.demconvention.com/speech/bill-clinton/, 9/5/2012

88   The DNC's Ridiculous attack on Mitt Romney's Social Security stance - http://www.washingtonpost.com/blogs/fact-checker/post/the-dncs-ridiculous-attack-on-mitt-romneys-social-security-stance/2011/10/05/gIQAsFHJOL_blog.html, Glenn Kessler, 10/06/2011

89   Fact Check: Obama and Romney on Social Security - http://abcnews.go.com/blogs/politics/2012/09/fact-check-obama-and-romney-on-social-security/, Jonathan Karl, 09/28/2012.

90   Kerry Picket, "Obama - 'If you've got a business – you didn't build that. Somebody else made that happen' ", *the Washington Times*, 7/15/12, http://www.washingtontimes.com/blog/watercooler

91   Emily Friedman, "Romney Likes 'Being Able to Fire People'", *ABC News*, 1/9/12, http://abcnews.go.com/blogs/politics/2012/01/romney-likes-being-able-to-fire-people/,

92   "Romney: 'I Like Being Able to Fire People'", *Associated Press*, 1/9/2012, http://www.youtube.com/watch?v=nBfWB64iHAs,

93   Michael Smerconish, "'You Didn't Build That' in Context," *The Blog*, 7/30/2012, http://www.huffingtonpost.com/michael-smerconish/you-didnt-build-that-in-c_b_1721794.html

94   2012 Talk Media, Inc , http://www.talkers.com/top-talk-radio-audiences/.

95   Joseph Gibson , "The Richest Politicians in America", *Celebrity Networth*, 8/13/2012, http://www.celebritynetworth.com/articles/entertainment-articles/10-richest-politicians-america/.

96   Political Salaries - http://www.infoplease.com/ipa/A0875856.html

97   Census.gov, http://www.census.gov/prod/2012pubs/p60-243.pdf

98   2012 Democratic National Convention Speeches- http://www.demconvention.com/speech/

99   Roe v. Wade - http://www.law.cornell.edu/supct/html/historics

100 "The Vietnam War: Seeds of Conflict 1945-1960", *The History Place*, http://www.historyplace.com/unitedstates/vietnam/index-1945.html

101 Howard Gleckman, "How Can 98% of Us Be Middle Class?", *Forbes*, 11/26/12, http://www.forbes.com/sites/beltway/2012/11/26/how-can-98-of-us-be-middle-class/.

102 John W. Schoen, "Who or what is the middle class?", *NBC News*, 10/17/07, http://www.msnbc.msn.com/id/21272238/ns/us_news-gut_check/t/who-or-what-middle-class/.

103 Peter Cohan, "What is Occupy Wall Street", *Forbes*, 10/10/11, http://www.forbes.com/sites/petercohan/2011/10/10/what-is-occupy-wall-street/.

104 Kay Bell, "Top 1 Percent: How much do they earn?", *Bankrate.com*, 10/24/11, http://www.bankrate.com/finance/taxes/top-1-percent-earn.aspx.

105 "The Forbes 400 The richest people in America", *Forbes*, 9/19/12, http://www.forbes.com/forbes-400/list/.

106 http://www.sarbanes-oxley-101.com/.

107 "Joseph P Kennedy", John F. Kennedy Presidential Library and Museum, Retrieved January 7, 2012.

108 Richard Austin Smith, "The Fifty-Million-Dollar Man: America's Biggest Fortunes", *Fortune,* 11/1/57.

109 U.S. Securities and Exchange Commission - http://www.sec.gov/about/sechistoricalsummary.htm.

110 http://en.wikipedia.org/wiki/Kennedy_family.

111 Adriana Gomez, "In campaign, Romney rarely notes Mexican heritage", *Deseret News*, 1/26/12, http://www.deseretnews.com/article/700219426/In-campaign-Romney-rarely-notes-Mexican-heritage.html?pg=2.

112 Tom Mahoney, *The Story of George Romney,* (Harper, 1960), 59–65.

113 T. George Harris, *Romney's Way,* (Garrett County Press, 2012), 91–92.

114 "American Motors Picks President and Chairman". *The New York Times.* October 13, 1954. http://query.nytimes.com/mem/archive/pdf?res=FB0 815F73B5B167B93C1A8178BD95F408585F9.

115 Sidney Fine, *Expanding the Frontiers of Civil Rights: Michigan, 1948-1968*, (Great Lakes Books, 2000), 216, 218.

116 Niraj Warikoo, "Mormon faith helped George Romney decide to run for governor of Michigan", *Detroit Free Press*, 1/30/12, http://www.freep.com/article/20120130/NEWS05/201300344/Mormon-faith-helped-George-Romney-decide-run-governor-Michigan.

117 Theodore H. White, *the Making of the President 1960,* (Harper Perennial, 2009), 37 reissue.

118 Hal Dardick and Joe Germuska, "Chicago aldermanic salaries, 2008-2012", *Chicago Tribune*, 01/30/12, http://media.apps.chicagotribune.com/tables/alderman-salaries.html.

119 Danny Garcia, "Bill Gates money: How much of it does he give away?", *moneyhowmuch.com*, 5/23/10, http://www.moneyhowmuch.com.

120 Tom Tugend, "Vegas billionaire Sheldon Adelson expected to set new charity donation record", *Jewish Journal*, 12/14/2006, http://www.jewishjournal.com/philanthropy

121 Gilbert Cruz, "Billionaire George Soros' Private Stimulus Plan", *Time*, 8/11/09, http://www.time.com/time/nation/article/0,8599,1915683,00.html.

122 Newsmax.com Staff, "Dick Cheney Donates Millions to Charity", *Newsmax.com*, 4/15/06, http://archive.newsmax.com/archives/ic/2006/4/15/02358.shtml.

123 Andrea Stone, "Mitt Romney Gives Millions To Charity, Most To Mormon Church", *Huffington Post*, 8/11/11, http://www.huffingtonpost.com/2011/08/11/mitt-romney-gives-million_n_924414.html.

124 United States presidential election of 1972, *Encyclopaedia Britannica*, http://www.britannica.com/EBchecked/topic/1582288/United-States-presidential-election-of-1972

125 United States presidential election of 1984, *Encyclopaedia Britannica*, http://www.britannica.com/EBchecked/topic/1575886/United-States-presidential-election-of-1984

126 United States presidential election of 1988, *Encyclopaedia Britannica*, http://www.britannica.com/EBchecked/topic/1575104/United-States-presidential-election-of-1988

127 United States presidential election of 1996, *Encyclopaedia Britannica*, http://www.britannica.com/EBchecked/topic/1573012/United-States-presidential-election-of-1996

128 United States presidential election of 2000, *Encyclopaedia Britannica*, http://www.britannica.com/EBchecked/topic/1570192/United-States-presidential-election-of-2000

129 United States presidential election of 2004, *Encyclopaedia Britannica*, http://www.britannica.com/EBchecked/topic/1570196/United-States-presidential-election-of-2004

130 United States presidential election of 2008, *Encyclopaedia Britannica*, http://www.britannica.com/EBchecked/topic/1335480/United-States-Presidential-Election-of-2008

131 Emily Coakley, "5 Most Controversial Presidential Elections in American History", *Finding Dulcinea*, 11/04/08, http://www.findingdulcinea.com/news/politics.

132 Pierre Tristam, "Complete Guide to the Abu Ghraib Photos and Torture Scandal", *About.com*

133 Highlights of the USA PATRIOT Act, Justice.gov, http://www.justice.gov

134 Al Franken, *Lies, and the Lying Liars Who Tell Them*, (Plume, 2004), 115

135 The USS Cole Bombing, *FBI.gov*, http://www.fbi.gov/about-us/history/famous-cases/uss-cole

136 Condoleezza Rice, 9/11 commission report, 4/8/04, http://www.cnn.com/2004/ALLPOLITICS/04/08/rice.transcript/

137 President Clinton, Joint Chiefs of Staff, CNN, 2/17/98, http://www.cnn.com/transcripts/clinton.iraq/.

138 Vicki Allen, "Congress Grants Bush War Powers Against Iraq", *Rense.com*, 10/11/2002, http://rense.com/general30/grant.htm

139 Richard D. Knabb, Jamie R. Rhome, and Daniel P. Brown, "Tropical Cyclone Report Hurricane Katrina", *National Hurricane Center*, 12/20/05, http://www.nhc.noaa.gov/pdf/TCR-AL122005_Katrina.pdf

140 Joe Kovacs, "School-buses showdown: Mayor Nagin vs. Russert", *WND WEEKLY*, 09/11/2005, HTTP://WWW.WND.COM/2005/09/32287/

141 NewsMax.com Staff, "Gov. Kathleen Blanco Refused Bush Aid", *NewsMax.com*, 9/4/05, http://archive.newsmax.com/archives/ic/2005/9/4/124905.shtml

142 Think Progress staff, "As Katrina Struck, Bush Vacationed", *ThinkProgress. org*, 8/30/05, http://thinkprogress.org/politics/2005/08/30/1683/as-katrina-struck-bush-vacated/?mobile=nc

143 Kent German, "Top 10 dot-com flops", *Cnet*, 11/13/90, http://www.cnet.com/1990-11136_1-6278387-1.html

144 Damian Paletta and Kara Scannell, "Ten Questions for Those Fixing the Financial Mess", *the Wall Street Journal*, 3/10/09. http://online.wsj.com/article/SB123665023774979341.html

145 http://www.foxnews.com/entertainment/2012/10/08/actress-stacey-dash-hit-with-racially-charged-attacks-after-endorsing-romney/

146 Carter G. Woodson, *the Mis-Education of the Negro*, (1933), p. 67

147 Transcript of Lincoln/ Douglas Fourth Debate: Charleston, Illinois, *National Park Service*, 9/18/1858, http://www.nps.gov/liho/historyculture/debate4.htm

148 Letter to Horace Greeley, *Abraham Lincoln Online*, 8/22/1862, http://www.abrahamlincolnonline.org/lincoln/speeches/greeley.htm

149 National Kids Count Program, "Children in single-parent families (percent) – 2011", the Annie E. Casey Foundation, http://datacenter.kidscount.org/data/acrossstates/Rankings.aspx?ind=106

150 http://www.cnn.com/election/2012/results/race/president

151 Miriam Hill, Andrew Seidman, and John Duchneskie, "In 59 Philadelphia voting divisions, Mitt Romney got zero votes", *the Inquirer*, 12/31/12, http://www.philly.com/philly/news/year-in-review/20121112_In_59_Philadelphia_voting_wards__Mitt_Romney_got_zero_votes.html

152 Mytheos Holt, "Odd? Romney Got ZERO Votes In 59 Precincts in Philly, and 9 Precincts in Ohio", *the Blaze*, 11/12/12, http://www.theblaze.com/stories/2012/11/12/odd-romney-got-zero-votes-in-59-precincts-in-philly-9-in-ohio/

153 "Races and Results, President: Full Results, Exit Polls", *CNN*, 12/10/12, http://www.cnn.com/election/2012/results/race/president

26707322R00146